Higher ENGLISH for CfE

PORTFOLIO WRITING SKILLS

Mary M. Firth and Andrew G. Ralston

SCOTTISH
EXAMINATION
MATERIALS

HODDER
GIBSON
AN HACHETTE UK COMPANY

Although every effort has been made to ensure that website addresses are correct at time of going to press, Hodder Gibson cannot be held responsible for the content of any website mentioned in this book. It is sometimes possible to find a relocated web page by typing in the address of the home page for a website in the URL window of your browser.

Hachette UK's policy is to use papers that are natural, renewable and recyclable products and made from wood grown in sustainable forests. The logging and manufacturing processes are expected to conform to the environmental regulations of the country of origin.

Orders: please contact Bookpoint Ltd, 130 Park Drive, Milton Park, Abingdon, Oxon OX14 4SE. Telephone: (44) 01235 827720. Fax: (44) 01235 400454. Lines are open 9.00–5.00, Monday to Saturday, with a 24-hour message answering service. Visit our website at www.hoddereducation.co.uk. Hodder Gibson can be contacted direct on: Tel: 0141 848 1609; Fax: 0141 889 6315; email: hoddergibson@hodder.co.uk

Cover photo © Getty Images / iStockphoto / Thinkstock
Illustrations by Peter Lubach at Redmoor Design
Typeset in 12/14.5pt Minion Regular by Integra Software Services Pvt. Ltd., Pondicherry, India
Printed in Spain

A catalogue record for this title is available from the British Library
ISBN: 978 1 4718 4861 2

CONTENTS

INTRODUCTION: WHAT DOES YOUR PORTFOLIO NEED?

Getting started

The task

You must compile a portfolio of two original pieces of writing. The portfolio will contribute 30 per cent of your total mark at Higher. Each piece is worth a maximum of 15 marks.

The aim

To gain as high a mark as possible in each of your two pieces of writing. It is possible to achieve full marks for writing of the highest quality.

Before you begin ... a word of warning!

The pieces of writing must be your own work. If you submit pieces that have been written in whole or in part by someone else, your entire award in English will be withheld and your awards in other subjects may also be in jeopardy.

Passing off the work of another person as your own is called plagiarism. This topic is looked at in more detail on pages 46–47, where you will be given more advice about what is and what is not considered plagiarism.

The Arrangements for Higher English permit 'reasonable assistance' in choosing your topics and suggestions for improving a first draft. Teachers and tutors are not allowed to rephrase for you, nor to provide key ideas or a plan, nor to correct particular errors of spelling and punctuation. There are no restrictions on the resources to which you may have access, however, such as spellcheckers and dictionaries.

You will have to sign a declaration that the work in your portfolio is all your own.

What kind of writing is expected in the portfolio?

The two pieces of writing required for the Higher English portfolio must be from the genres identified in the groups below. One should be from group A and one from group B.

- Group A (broadly creative): a personal essay, a reflective essay, or an imaginative piece.
- Group B (broadly discursive): an argumentative essay, a persuasive essay, or a report for a specified purpose.

Understanding the genres

Broadly creative writing

You may choose from two distinct types of creative writing: personal/reflective or imaginative writing (prose, drama or poetry).

In a **personal/reflective** piece of writing, you present your thoughts, feelings and opinions. You draw from your own personal experience in expressing and illustrating your views.

The aim is to interest and entertain the reader.

Imaginative. Some writing comes purely from your imagination. You might choose to write a **short story**, but you might also consider writing a **poem** (or a thematically linked set of poems) or a **drama script**. It is also acceptable to write a 'chapter' of a novel – there is no need to write the whole novel! For imaginative writing, you have an unlimited range of topics from which to choose.

The aim is to entertain and enthrall the reader.

Broadly discursive writing

Discursive writing may be argumentative or persuasive, or may take the form of a report.

In an **argumentative** piece of writing, you evaluate two or more viewpoints on a subject in a balanced manner.

The aim is to inform and enlighten the reader and to help them reach a view.

In a **persuasive** piece of writing, you make a strong case for something you believe in – rather like a lawyer.

The aim is to influence the reader's opinion.

A **report** is a factual piece of writing that presents information on a topic you have researched in clear, continuous, formal prose.

A good report will organise material logically from a variety of sources, including spoken and graphic ones.

The aim is to inform the reader.

Choosing a topic

Will I get a list of topics to choose from?

It is up to you to choose the topics for your writing pieces. The SQA does not provide a list of topics.

In the past, candidates for Higher English wrote under exam conditions and were given a short list of topics from which to choose.

This system of assessing a candidate's ability was abandoned; it was considered unsatisfactory for several reasons:

- Firstly, the limited time available meant that candidates who had good ideas might not manage to develop them fully. For example, a promising story might be submitted with no ending, or with an unsatisfactory one.

Help! I can't finish this in time! It'll have to all be a dream!

- Secondly, it might be that none of the topics appealed to a candidate. Candidates might have had interests and enthusiasms that they were given no chance to reveal.

I can't think of what to write on any of these topics! Last year's were better!

'A Football Match'. Great! I'll write about that.

- Thirdly, markers often found that many candidates would choose the same question. In some cases – particularly in argumentative essays – candidates had little chance to impress markers by being original. In addition, they had no opportunity to research a topic or check that their facts were accurate when exploring a discursive topic.

The best topic for you

It is important to be aware of your own strengths. You are likely to write well if you:

- write about something you know
- write about something that genuinely interests you
- enjoy what you are writing.

Try the following questionnaire. Once you have completed it, you may find you have revealed various topics that would yield good pieces of writing.

What do you know about?

Your life experiences

Think about the things that have happened in your own life so far. Write down brief headings representing experiences that were good or special in some way. These might include being in a winning team, performing in a play or taking part in a family event such as the birth of a new baby. Try to think of at least six things.

1
2
3
4
5
6

Now, think about things that were not so good. For example, a big disappointment, a car accident or a quarrel with a friend. Write down six headings that represent these moments.

1
2
3
4
5
6

Look back at your lists. Think again about these episodes in your life. Now, rank them in the order that you think they would be most interesting to write – and to read – about.

People

Think about the people who have been important in your life: your family, friends and acquaintances. Think about relationships that have been important to you. Write down the names of two people about whom you might find it interesting to write.

1
2

Knowledge

Think about the things of which you have special knowledge. These might include a sport or hobby, or a place where you often go on holiday, or even the place where you live.

Many candidates insist they have no special knowledge of anything!

Everyone knows a lot about their school however or their home town, or keeping a pet. Write down headings for all the special knowledge which you can think of.

1
2
3
4

Now rank these, putting the subject you have most knowledge about first.

Opinions

Think of things about which you feel strongly. Usually, people feel more strongly about negative opinions than positive ones, but either can make an interesting and involving topic to write about.

Firstly, look at the list of statements below and give your opinion about each a rating from one to seven as indicated in this table:

1	2	3	4	5	6	7
Very strongly disagree	Definitely disagree	Tend to disagree	Neutral – have no feelings	Tend to agree	Definitely agree	Very strongly agree

Statement	My rating
a) It is much harder being a teenager today than it was when my parents were young.	
b) Society is still very unfair: rich people get all the breaks and the poor get nothing.	
c) Politicians are all out for what they can get. They don't really want to serve the public; they are just ambitious for power and money.	
d) Being old is awful – I would hate to be old.	
e) Winning the lottery would be the best thing that could happen to me.	
f) It is just another form of racism when Scottish people say they hate the English. The World Cup t-shirts with the slogan 'Anyone but England' should have been banned.	
g) Children who commit terrible crimes (like those who murdered the toddler Jamie Bulger) should not be treated like adult criminals, but should instead get help.	
h) Most people will bully others if they get the chance.	
i) I would love to be famous. Being famous would be brilliant.	
j) What people look like is very important.	

Now, compare your ratings with others in your class or group. Identify the topics that aroused the strongest feelings, and discuss the reasons for this.

Next, write down a list of topics about which you feel strongly. You could include some of the topics in the box above, or add other ideas of your own.

Some suggestions

Although no topics are set and you are free to choose your own subjects within the limits set by the examiners, the list of suggested topics in **Part Three** may help you to form some ideas on what to write about.

What the markers are looking for

How can I be sure of getting a good mark?

Firstly, the marker will check that your writing is of the required degree of technical accuracy. According to the marking instructions, 'consistent technical accuracy' is required for a pass mark (8 or above) at Higher. Your writing will then be evaluated and marked according to two criteria – content and style – and how far it demonstrates the following features (as appropriate to your chosen genre):

	All pieces of writing	Creative	Discursive
Content	• Committed attention to purpose and audience.	• Strong creative qualities. • Command of the genre. • Clearly introduced and developed themes. • Maturity, self-awareness and insight in exploring feelings, ideas and experiences. • Strong sense of writer's personality.	• Full understanding of and engagement with ideas. • Evidence of full research and appropriate selection from it. • Clear and sustained line of thought.
Style	• Skilful use of the linguistic features of the chosen genre. • Confident and varied expression. • Effective structure.		

What if the marker doesn't like my piece of writing? People have different tastes.

Markers are trained to be objective. However, certain content should be avoided. Creative writing that contains violence or explicit sexual references may offend, as can the use of bad language. Similarly, the expression of extreme views regarding race or religion might also be deemed unacceptable. Deliberately aiming to shock in one of these ways is not advisable. The marker is likely to be someone like your teacher; if you feel your writing would be acceptable to your teacher, then you're unlikely to have any problems.

> I've often wondered how teachers give marks to writing pieces. Isn't it difficult to decide what mark to give?

That is a good question! English teachers are often asked how they decide what mark to give a piece of work.

Markers compare a candidate's piece of writing with a list of features described in their marking instructions, and assign it to a broad category depending on which features best match what has been achieved in the piece. They then decide where to place it within the range of marks available in that category.

You may view these marking instructions and the lists of features which comprise these criteria on the SQA website: www.sqa.org.uk/files_ccc/GAInfoHigherEnglish.pdf.

SQA markers work according to some general principles:

- They are asked to mark positively. Thus, they always look for the strengths in your writing and marks are accumulated accordingly, rather than deducted for particular errors or omissions.

- Markers are also instructed to mark holistically. This means that they consider each piece as a whole. Although they assess each piece on content and style, these are not treated separately for the purposes of marking; it is the general impression which is all important.

Finally, keep in mind this encouraging quotation from the SQA document:

> 'Writing does not have to be perfect to gain full marks.'

> I'd like my writing to be in the 'excellent' or 'very good' category, but I'm still not sure how to achieve this!

The aim of this book is to give advice on how to ensure your writing is as good as it can possibly be!

- You will be deconstructing pieces of writing and looking at how to craft elements like openings, dialogue, linkage, endings and various technical literary devices.

- You will be asked to think about planning and redrafting.

- You will be encouraged to look at examples of professional writing and to think about how they achieve their impact.

- You will also be encouraged to look at examples of other students' work and to consider how it might be improved.

- You will analyse your own strengths and abilities in writing in order to choose the best topics for you.

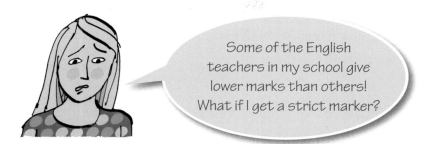

Some of the English teachers in my school give lower marks than others! What if I get a strict marker?

The SQA operates a moderation procedure. Markers are given examples of writing that, in the opinion of the SQA, would fall into each of the marking categories. Your work will be compared against these examples (known as exemplars). Marked work is also sampled and checked, so that the SQA can be sure all their markers are assessing work fairly and accurately. So you can be assured that your writing will be given a fair chance.

What's the difference between a Higher and a National 5 portfolio?

If you previously completed a National 5 English course, you will already have produced a portfolio of Creative and Discursive writing.

Higher English allows you to improve the skills you learnt at National 5 level. A greater degree of complexity, maturity and sophistication is expected at Higher.

To help you understand these different expectations, there is a section headed 'From National 5 to Higher' at the end of each part of this book.

Finally, remember that a marker is likely to be marking a hundred or more pieces of writing. What is likely to make yours stand out as belonging to a top category? What is likely to see it relegated to a low one?

For discussion

In groups, look at this list of features that might influence a marker either positively or negatively. Rank them in order of importance.

Positive features	Negative features
A topic that stands out as different from all the others.	Saying nothing new about a very common topic.
A sense of a bright, funny, pleasant personality in the writer.	A personal experience that is mainly narrative.
A gripping or moving personal story.	A discussion that is disjointed and lacks a clear argument.
Fiction that is readable and genuinely entertaining.	A story that reads as if copied from somewhere else.
A clear, well-structured argument.	Too many long words – the 'swallowed a dictionary' effect.
Fluent, clear writing with good word choice.	Monotonous writing with repetitive sentence structures and repetition of words.

Which features could you aim to include in your personal list of dos and don'ts? Compile your own list.

Length

How long must my pieces of writing be?

Length is reckoned by the number of words used. If you are working on a computer, you can check this quickly and easily by clicking on Word Count (usually found under the Review tab).

Maximum: 1,300 words

The word limit is 1,300, but there is no need to use the maximum allowed. Full marks can be achieved by a shorter piece, if it is appropriate to purpose.

You must take care to avoid exceeding 1,300 words. The word count may exclude titles, footnotes and lists of sources, but must include any quotations.

Presentation

Writing that is submitted for the portfolio should be word processed or neatly handwritten on one side of the page only. Pages should be clearly numbered. Legibility is of paramount importance. It is not advisable to use circles – or hearts! – to dot the letter 'i' when handwriting. Do not use pencil and avoid bright colours, particularly pink or red, since red is used to mark scripts. Avoid elaborate fonts when word processing, such as those which imitate handwriting.

The following conventions are recommended:

- A standard font: Times New Roman or Arial are good options
- Point size: 12
- Alignment: left or justified
- Margins: 2cm all round
- Line spacing: 1.5 or 2
- Print colour: black (except possibly for graphs, diagrams, etc. in a report).

Check, check, check…

You must strive to achieve the 'consistent technical accuracy' which is a requirement for Higher portfolio writing. Use a spellchecker and/or a dictionary to help eliminate errors. Always read over your final draft or print-out carefully in case you have made an error the spellchecker won't pick up, such as using the wrong version of a word (e.g. off/of) or missing out a word.

Keeping to the rules

On page v, you were told that your writing must be your own work, and that you must sign a declaration to confirm this.

As evidence, your teacher or tutor will ensure that you provide four pieces of documentation for each of your two portfolio pieces:

- A draft title and proposals
- An outline plan
- Your first draft
- Your final version.

You are recommended to keep a log of your progress. You should put a date on each stage, and also record the comments made by your teacher or tutor on both the outline plan and your first draft. A template for such a log can be found at the end of this book. You may wish to do a further draft before your final version, but remember that the Arrangements say that the number of drafts 'should not normally exceed two'.

Sources

Don't forget to add your sources! For your discursive writing piece, you must make a list of all the sources you have consulted. These can be added as footnotes or in a list at the end of your piece of writing. You must give clear details, such as the dates and writers of newspaper articles, specific addresses for web pages, and book titles and their dates of publication.

Always keep a record of these details as you research your topic. It can be very frustrating and time-consuming if you have to go back and track down your sources later. If you have not consulted any sources, you must say so.

For full guidance on all aspects of the Higher for CfE English course, take a look at the 'Course Assessment Specification' document on the SQA website: www.sqa.org.uk/sqa/47904.html.

PART ONE

BROADLY CREATIVE WRITING
PERSONAL/REFLECTIVE WRITING

One of the two pieces of writing for your portfolio must be creative. For a creative piece, you may choose to write on a personal/reflective topic or to produce a piece of fiction in the form of prose, drama, or poetry.

Getting started

It is a good idea to base your writing on your own experience, for the simple reason that if you have experienced something you will know better than anyone else how you felt and thought about it.

This is a view shared by many famous authors:

'the best writing is always the most painful personal wrung-out tossed from cradle warm protective mind-tap…'

(Jack Kerouac)

'Stick to your story. It is not the most important subject in history but it is one about which you are uniquely qualified to speak.'

(Evelyn Waugh)

What the examiner is looking for

- A sense of your own personality.

- Expression of your thoughts and feelings, not just a narrative account. As well as giving an account of an experience, you must reflect on it.

- An entertaining treatment of the topic: originality and perhaps humour.

- An appropriate style. An informal, chatty style may be more suitable than a formal one. Remember, however, that a conversational style must be controlled with careful and accurate punctuation.

In this section of the book, we'll look at what professional writers have to say about two of the topics for personal/reflective writing that everyone can relate to in some way: 'Great escapes: where I go when it's all too much' and 'Decisions'. Each extract is followed by some questions to help you understand the techniques used by the writer.

By the end of this section, you should have picked up some tips from these authors that you can apply to your own writing.

Great escapes: where I go when it's all too much

Reading a good book, pinned to the bed by a sleeping cat, shopping with friends ... four writers describe where they find relief from stress and anxiety.

Julie Myerson

Author and journalist

A few years ago I was rushed to hospital with heart palpitations. Or, at least, my GP agreed that my heart was beating way too fast to be acceptable and sent me off to Casualty to be looked at.

Of course, if your heart is beating rapidly it's unlikely to calm down in an A&E department. By the time the doctors had surrounded me, taped wires to my chest and frowned at my pulse, my heart rate had soared. After a few minutes I was told that I wasn't about to have a heart attack (as I'd feared), that it was probably just panic, that the best thing to do was relax and watch my heart rate drop. Easy for them to say.

So I shut my eyes. Even though I felt stressed and afraid, I knew I had to relax. I took deep breaths and tried to think of something calm and serene. I took myself to a desert-island-style beach: blue skies, palm trees, the kind of holiday-brochure place you're supposed to go when you meditate. It didn't work. I have no relationship with such beaches. So I tried my adored Suffolk coastline. Vast grey skies, grey choppy sea, a sense of infinity that always brings death to mind. Not good for my heartbeat. I came back with a bump.

I tried thinking of my kids. Which made me happy and warm, yes, but not calm. In the end, I was surprised by the two things that worked.

One: I am lying pinned to a bed by a cat, which is on my stomach, purring gently. Now, I swear I'm not one of those mad cat-ladies – give me people over animals any day – but you try remaining tense when the family tabby has decided to lie on you. Your limbs get heavy, you submit. Cats settle you. They don't take no for an answer. I conjured this picture and I felt warm and still. My heartbeat began to slow. →

Two: my childhood bed. Or one particular view of the sheet. Striped pale pink, lavender, yellow, blue (didn't all we 1960s children have these sheets?), slightly furred from many washes, tucked tightly around my shoulders. A child's-eye view of these sheets brings thermometers and penicillin to mind, long days of watching the sun move around the room, of knowing you were looked after, safe. This, too, brought down my heartbeat.

The men in white coats came and discharged me. I was pronounced fit, if tense. So began a long struggle to relax. But I discovered something interesting on that bed in Casualty. For me, escape is not to a place but to a feeling. It's not about choice but about no choice. The tabby cat pins you down, the childhood bed sheets are tightly tucked. You're not going anywhere.

Your heartbeat plummets and you are calm.

© The Times / News Syndication

Questions

1. Julie Myerson opens with a short account of a personal experience. What is the connection between this and the main theme of the article?
2. Read paragraph three again. What do you notice about the sentence lengths here?
3. Which methods of relaxation didn't work for her?
4. Find one sentence that sums up the most important thing the writer discovered about relaxation as a result of her hospital experience.

Kathy Lette

Author

The good thing about being a woman is that no matter how bad things get, we can always go shopping. Armani who art in heaven, Hallowed be thy name.

I once read an article that said that typical symptoms of stress are eating too much, impulse buying and driving too fast. Are they kidding? That's my idea of a divine day. Is there anything better than losing yourself in rack-pawing, sales delirium and guiltless gimme-gimme while gossiping with girlfriends about each other's marriages? How we cackle. How we roar.

I know that men would rather listen to a Yoko Ono CD than go shopping. But it has been scientifically proven that no woman can walk past a shoe shop that is having a sale and not go in. It's the greatest difference between the sexes. Besides the fact that we're so superior. (Why do men like intelligent women? Because opposites attract.) To top off our perfect afternoon, it's champagne cocktails in the bar, then home to complain to your long-suffering bloke that you didn't want to go shopping – but the others made you.

© The Times / News Syndication

Questions

1 This extract is written as if Kathy Lette is talking directly to the reader. Quote two examples of this.
2 Find an example of how she is making fun of (a) men, (b) women and (c) herself.
3 How would you describe the tone of this passage?

Simon Barnes

Chief sports writer, *The Times*

I have an escape that is fast, dangerous and unpredictable. It requires hard work and it consumes a fair amount of money. I don't seek this for therapeutic reasons: therapy is an incidental benefit. I do it because living any other way is unthinkable. I live with horses.

There are four of them at home now. I ride two and do the feeding and mucking out for the lot. I have horses, I ride horses, I care for horses because … well, because it's what I do.

Part of the attraction is in contrast. A writer spends a lot of time inside his own head: with horses, if you are not concentrating on externals, you are going to get hurt. But it is not the whole story.

With horses, I'm not escaping from the pressure of work. It's much better than that: I am escaping from the pressure of being human.

Questions

1 Do you notice anything unusual about the way the first paragraph is structured?
2 In your own words, explain the satisfaction Simon Barnes gets from looking after horses.

Hannah Betts

Journalist, *The Times*

Perhaps my escape is too obvious – too mainstream a refuge – but there are times when nothing, but nothing, is as real and restorative as fiction.

Conventional modes of retreat do nothing for me. I find relaxing stressful, care little for nature, have no god and, gregarious as I can make myself, must balance bouts of socialising with bookish seclusion. Reading is life's consummate pleasure. But there are occasions when it is a breathe-into-a-paper-bag necessity: commutes when I can't stomach a newspaper;

→

weekends when I am sick and tired of everyone and everything. Times when I need to be 'in my head' but, finding my head an over-wrought and over-stuffed thing, prefer to seek solace in someone else's.

Doubtless this is why travel invariably leaves me cold: I've been to better places.

© The Times / News Syndication

Questions

1   State three methods of relaxation that did not help Hannah Betts.
2   What do you think she means by the last sentence?

Thinking it over...

Check your understanding and appreciation of these extracts by filling in the table below.

	Julie Myerson	Kathy Lette	Simon Barnes	Hannah Betts
The writer's preferred method of escape				
Ways in which it helps him/her relax or escape				
How effective is the opening sentence/paragraph in catching the reader's attention?				
Examples of interesting and effective word choice				
Any other features of the style of writing that you noticed (for example, sentence structure, paragraphing, punctuation, etc.)				
Your opinion of each extract: Which do you like best? Why?				
Is there anything the writers did that you could do in your own writing (without simply copying them)?				

For practice

Reading about these writers' ways of escaping should stimulate you to write a similar piece in which you describe your means of relaxation.

- Talk to a partner about situations you find stressful. Describe the ways you escape from these; discuss why your methods work for you, and how they change your thoughts and feelings.

- Jot down your findings in random note form.

- Then try to put your thoughts into a more logical sequence. If you find this difficult, you could follow a similar paragraph plan to the one used in Julie Myerson's piece:

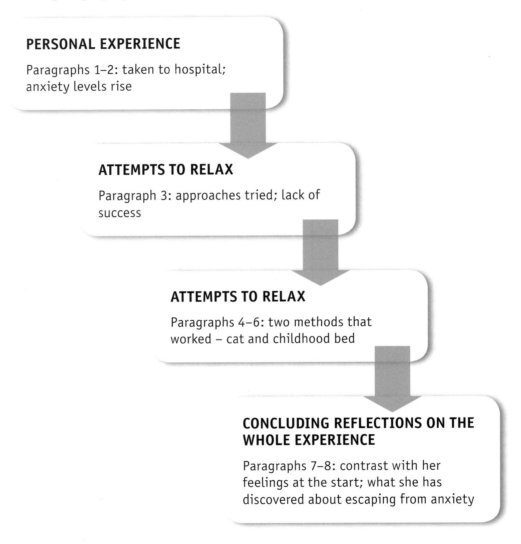

PERSONAL EXPERIENCE

Paragraphs 1–2: taken to hospital; anxiety levels rise

ATTEMPTS TO RELAX

Paragraph 3: approaches tried; lack of success

ATTEMPTS TO RELAX

Paragraphs 4–6: two methods that worked – cat and childhood bed

CONCLUDING REFLECTIONS ON THE WHOLE EXPERIENCE

Paragraphs 7–8: contrast with her feelings at the start; what she has discovered about escaping from anxiety

Note that this kind of writing generally involves a combination of narrative, description, discussion and reflection.

- Narrative: relate a past incident that made you feel anxious or pressurised and from which you needed to escape.

- Description: describe the steps you took to relax – whether these were in your imagination or involved physically going somewhere else.

- Discussion: analyse how the method of escape worked and the effects it had on you.

- Reflection: look back on the process; compare how you felt afterwards with how you felt at the beginning. What have you learned? Have you been able to apply this lesson on other occasions?

The right style

- A first-person ('I') approach is most suitable for a piece of writing of this type.

- As the 'Escape' extracts show, there are different ways of starting. Julie Myerson begins in a narrative way, by recounting a personal experience; Kathy Lette and Hannah Betts begin with a topic sentence stating their method of escape; Simon Barnes begins with suspense and waits until the end of the first paragraph before saying 'I live with horses'.

- There are different ways of ending, but most of the extracts finish with a short sentence or paragraph summing up the writer's positive feelings.

- Make a list of adjectives that would describe your various feelings. If necessary, use a thesaurus to find alternative words.

- In order to convey your feelings, try to draw parallels and make comparisons – but bear in mind George Orwell's advice (see page 36): 'Never use a metaphor, simile or other figure of speech which you are used to seeing in print.'

- Vary your sentence lengths and sentence structures. (See pages 32–33 for help with this.)

- Leave your first draft aside for 24 hours, then come back to it and revise it.

Decisions

We are all faced with choices and decisions on a daily basis. Some are minor but some turn out to have far-reaching consequences.

Paul Tillich (1886–1965), the German-born philosopher and theologian, wrote: 'Decision is a risk rooted in the courage of being free.'

The singer and composer Bob Marley (1945–81) said: 'Every man gotta right to decide his own destiny.'

Here are two pieces of writing to help you think about the question of decision-making.

'The Road Not Taken'

This famous poem was written by Robert Frost, an American poet of the early twentieth century.

Two roads diverged in a yellow wood,
And sorry I could not travel both
And be one traveller, long I stood
And looked down one as far as I could
5   To where it bent in the undergrowth;

Then took the other, as just as fair,
And having perhaps the better claim,
Because it was grassy and wanted wear;
Though as for that the passing there
10   Had worn them really about the same,
And both that morning equally lay

In leaves no step had trodden black.
Oh, I kept the first for another day!
Yet knowing how way leads on to way,
15   I doubted if I should ever come back.
I shall be telling this with a sigh
Somewhere ages and ages hence:
Two roads diverged in a wood, and I –
I took the one less travelled by,
20   And that has made all the difference.

Think about the poem (1): the meaning

- What did the traveller feel about having to choose between two roads?

- What was different about the roads?

- What was similar about them?

- What made the choice difficult?

- What did he intend to do on some future occasion?

- Why was he unlikely to be able to do this?

- Which of the following best explains the meaning of the last line?

    a) We can't tell what effect this choice had on him.
    b) He made the right choice.
    c) He made the wrong choice.
    d) He made a choice that affected the rest of his life.

Think about the poem (2): the style

This poem has both a literal and a metaphorical meaning.

On a literal level it describes: _____

On a metaphorical level it is about: _____

'What Might Have Been'

Children's writer Anne Fine looks back over her career and considers some of the different paths she might have taken in life.

In Robert Frost's poem 'The Road Not Taken', the poet wistfully looks back at choices he could so easily have made, lives he could so easily have found himself living. In spite of the fact that everyone who knows me falls about laughing at the notion, I've always been convinced I could have been, not a writer slouching all day at a desk, but someone fit and sharp, perfectly tuned: a trapeze artist, maybe; or a high-wire walker.

The utter conviction began the day I lost – and found – the key to the garage. Behind our house was a cul-de-sac with five brick garages with wooden doors. One day, when I was about six, I was sent to fetch back the little silver key from ours. All I remember is strolling back and swinging the key round and round on its short loop of string. And suddenly it had flown off my finger and was sailing back over my shoulder to land somewhere – anywhere – in the straggling, uncut grass.

I was horrified. I knew nothing of locksmiths, spare keys, bolt-cutters. I think I must have assumed the very, very six-year-old worst – that the garage would stay locked for ever. We would never again get at anything inside it. And my father, without the car on which his job depended, would lose his position overnight.

➜

I must have half died from terror. I can't imagine what I thought would happen to me. But I know this. I would have traded practically anything in the world to have had the key safely back in my hand.

I didn't move. Standing stock-still, I made a bargain with the deity that I'd be good all my life if only I could find it. Still rooted to the spot, I reached down and scrabbled round for a stone the same weight as the key, and hurled it upwards in the exact same perfect arc in which I'd watched the key sail over my head a few moments earlier. The instant the stone was out of my hand, I spun round to watch where it fell. To this day it's hard to believe I really did hear that tell-tale clink of stone on metal. But I did.

I'm sure I did try to be good for a while. But, deep inside, I didn't truly believe I'd had help from the heavens. Instead, I came to believe I had some physical form of what musicians call 'perfect pitch': the absolute bodily judgement you see brought to perfection in top-flight athletes, crack shots and prima ballerinas.

A road quite definitely not taken! For even as far back as secondary school, I took against the complications of exercises and sport: fixed times, the right gear, partners, rules… But, once or twice since, I've been reminded of what could have been. When I was ten, my uncle took me shooting. I wouldn't dream of trying to shoot any wild creature now; and even back then it can't have crossed my mind that I might actually have hit anything or I'd have handed the gun back.

But shoot I did, dutifully following my uncle's orders, raising the rifle and taking careful aim.

Whatever it was, I nearly killed it. Don't ask me how he knew. Maybe he saw some leaf blown off beside his left ear. But in any case, he was astonished. It was a lucky escape – both for me and for the creature.

Another time, in my first job, I strolled along to the staff trampoline club simply to wait for my lift home. 'Have a go', everyone insisted. I climbed up, bounced up high, spun into a ball, revolved, unfolded at exactly the right moment, and landed faultlessly before shooting up into the next bounce. No one would believe I'd never been on a trampoline before. I expected, till I left, they all thought I was a liar.

So here I sit, fifty and idle, still secretly believing I have a hidden, almost unused, gift, and deep inside me is a spangled figure weaving faultless figures of eight through air sixty feet above sawdust. At fifteen, there are so many people you might become. At fifty, so many you might have been. That's why that oh-so-deceptively simple little poem of Robert Frost's is one of the world's great favourites.

One of mine as well.

Giving it a structure

There are several lessons we can learn from the way Anne Fine has written this piece.

Notice how she develops her thoughts on this topic, combining narrative and reflection.

Paragraph	Purpose	Content
1	Introduction	Refers to poem and to roads she might have taken
2–3	Narrative	Story of lost key
4–6	Reflection	How she reacted to this
7–9	Narrative	Reference back to 'The Road Not Taken'; shooting incident
10	Narrative	Third example: trampoline
11	Reflection	Reference back to poem
12	Conclusion	One-sentence paragraph

Reflecting on the experience

Reflective writing contains some narrative elements, but primarily it explores the writer's thoughts and feelings about the experience, rather than simply telling us what happens.

Select three incidents referred to in Anne Fine's article. Describe her feelings about each one. Then write down the words and phrases that show these feelings, and try to identify any other techniques she used to help the reader understand how she felt at the time, or later on in life.

Incident	What she feels about the incident	Techniques used to express her feelings (for example, word choice, sentence structure, imagery, etc.)
1		
2		
3		

For practice

- Talk to a partner about a time in your life when you had to make a choice or decision.
- How did you make up your mind?
- Did the choice or decision have consequences for you, or for others?
- Looking back on it, do you think or feel differently now? Do you think you made the right choice?

Writing task

Now use these thoughts to write your own piece on either of the two topics discussed in this chapter: 'Great escapes' or 'Decisions'. For guidance on other suitable subjects for personal/reflective writing, see pages 73–75.

If you find it difficult to put your thoughts into order, try drawing up a paragraph plan, such as this spider diagram for the 'Decisions' topic:

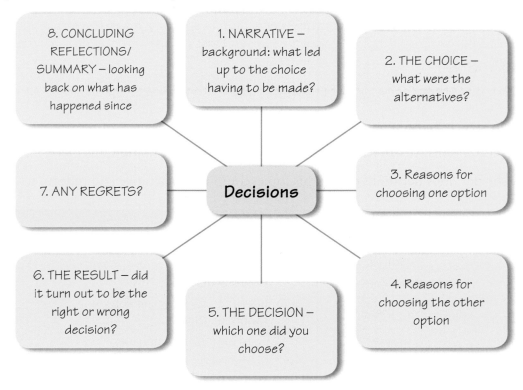

From National 5 to Higher

A piece of personal/reflective writing at Higher will exhibit the following strengths:

- It will contain less narrative and more reflection. Narrative passages are included to provide a context for the reflection. Commenting on a piece of writing which gained full marks, SQA markers noted that 'a particular strength is that there is no "narrative" as such'.

- Narrative and reflection will be integrated, rather than dealt with separately. Another marker liked one piece because 'reflection is embedded in the narrative'.

- Feelings will not merely be stated but will be explored in depth. For example, the writer might question his or her motives; he or she might probe more deeply into feelings with great honesty, admitting that these feelings are conflicting or confused.

- A strong sense of the writer's personality will be conveyed. At the same time, the writer should be able to stand back from the event and look at 'self' in a more detached way. SQA markers praised one reflective piece because 'self-awareness permeates the essay'.

- It will approach the limit of 1,300 words (depending on the chosen genre).

By contrast, if a personal/reflective piece exhibits features such as the following, it is likely to be too simple for Higher level:

- The feelings/ideas/experiences explored lack maturity and full engagement.

- The exploration and development of feelings/ideas/experiences is limited.

- It tends to separate narrative and reflection, rather than skilfully integrating them.

- The sense of the writer's personality is rather limited.

- It falls considerably short of 1,300 words (depending on the chosen genre).

How good is it?

According to SQA examiners, a piece of personal/reflective writing that would gain top marks in Higher English will be characterised by:

…ideas/feelings/experiences which are explored with a strong degree of mature reflection/self-awareness/involvement/insight/sensitivity. The approach taken will clearly reveal the writer's personality.

In assessing how good a piece of personal/reflective writing is, remember the following points made in this chapter:

- Personal/reflective writing is not the same as narrative writing, although it may have narrative elements in it.
- It should convey a sense of your personality.
- It should concentrate on thoughts and feelings rather than on events.
- There should be some kind of development. Reflection means looking back. You might, for example, explain how your attitude to something has changed with the passage of time.

Bearing this in mind, read the following two reflective pieces written by Higher English students. Imagine you are the marker and discuss how well written you think they are. The questions at the end of each essay will help you to do this.

Then decide what mark you would award each piece out of 15 and write your own marker's comment in the box.

Sample answer 1: Rebecca's reflective essay

Topic: 'Great escapes: where I go when it's all too much'

Running

When the hectic hustle and bustle of everyday life gets to me, I run. When I feel angry or exasperated, I run. When I want to escape any anxieties and problems, I run. When I argue with my friends and family, I run. Even when I feel tired and weary, I run.

The instant I pull on my familiar, tatty trainers I can feel the tension begin to lessen. As I warm up physically, I calm down mentally in anticipation of my run. When I step outside, I do not need to think, I switch to automatic pilot and am drawn, as if by an invisible force, to the park.

I hear the comforting, regular beat of my trainers on the gravel under my feet. The familiar crunching noise as I stride over it lulls my mind. Step by step I glide into my rhythm and start to relax. The beat becomes softer as my feet hit smooth tarmac.

I gradually become aware of my breathing. In for two, out for two, in for two, out for two. Over and over. My face is becoming increasingly hot, but as I increase my pace, the wind whips pleasantly around me, cooling me down. I am in total control. I am inexorable.

I arrive at the traffic lights – fleetingly irritated at the interruption – and press the button. I can hear the cars speeding past me as I wait for the green man. I am already more calm and relaxed than I was before I set out and my feet subconsciously continue to pound the pavement – anxious not to lose the momentum. Suddenly the green man glares in my face and I am back to concentrating solely on my running.

In for two, out for two, in for two, out for two.

The soothing rhythm clears my brain and as I turn into the park I feel free and weightless. The adrenaline courses round my body and I feel I could run forever. Other runners pass by but I am oblivious. My mind is empty; I have only one thought – keep running.

I see the steep hill ahead. I bring my knees up higher as I prepare myself for the challenge that looms before me. I can hear my heart beat harder, faster, louder. I can feel the blood pounding through my ears as I push myself on. My breathing rate increases and becomes noisy and laboured. Nearly there, keep going, nearly at the top. My legs begin to feel heavy and my muscles scream with pain. My lungs are about to explode, but I keep on running. I can think of nothing else. Just as I feel I can go no further, I reach the top.

I pause momentarily and take a deep, triumphant breath. As I start the descent my stride lengthens and the pain in my muscles subsides. My breathing and heart rate slow and, all too quickly, I am at the bottom.

I enter the woods and the atmosphere changes. Sounds are muffled by the trees overhead and I am running in a vacuum. The ground is soft and slightly wet underfoot. All is quiet except for the sound of my breathing and the occasional snap of a twig. As the aroma of damp undergrowth fills my nostrils I feel totally relaxed. In for two, out for two, in for two, out for two. I concentrate on my breathing as I enter deeper into the woods. Darkness enfolds me as the trees block out all sunlight, but my head is clear and bright.

➜

The sunlight hits me like a fist in the face as I exit the woods. I hear the soft, cushioned, rhythmical thud of my trainers on the grass. I am running alongside a fast-flowing stream that seems to be racing me along the bank, mocking me. I quicken my pace and force myself to keep going. The sun is beating down hard on the back of my neck. I can feel its warmth against my body. I feel truly alive and invigorated.

As I turn a corner, I can at last see the gate. I am back on the tarmac and the sound of my feet against the ground has once again become clear. I force myself to pick up the pace as I head for home. I can see my house, just a couple of hundred metres away. By now I'm sprinting full pelt and racing myself home, no longer caring about my breathing or stride pattern. All I am thinking about is my destination.

I arrive home a different person.

Questions

1   How interesting did you find the subject matter?
2   Did the personality of the writer come through?
3   Was there any humour?
4   How was the piece of writing structured?
5   Was there development in the writer's thoughts/feelings?
6   How successfully were narrative, descriptive and reflective elements combined?
7   Which stylistic features were used to good effect? (For example, word choice, sentence structure, imagery, repetition or any other techniques.)

Task

Mark awarded: _____/15

Marker's comment:

Sample answer 2: Laura's reflective essay

Topic: 'Great escapes: where I go when it's all too much'

My addiction in three stages

I am a junkie. I freely admit it. Going a day without it is hard; the minutes pass by like hours, stretching like elastic to produce the maximum amount of boredom. It has become second nature to me, part of my daily routine. Eat, drink and log on. That's right, I'm a net junkie.

Now please don't make a common misinterpretation. I am a net junkie, not, I hasten to add, a computer geek. I could find a record that was limited to 1,000 copies and distributed only in Alaska, but don't ask me why the computer crashed.

→

It began, as most addictions do, from something smaller and almost harmless. As a drug addict moves on from speed to heroin, I moved on from Garbage to the internet. This may not be an obvious connection, but the day I saw Garbage live changed my life. I wanted to know everything about this wonder-band and the superwoman who was the lead singer, and the internet was an obvious place to start. I found websites devoted to them, I spent hours poring over interview after interview online. That was stage one, using the internet to find information.

Stage two began also as a result of Garbage. Through my search for knowledge I discovered message boards. These to me were some sort of heaven. I could post questions, find facts, share an obsession. From them I traded live CDs across the Atlantic and formed a pen-pal allegiance with a boy in Brazil. Yes, message boards opened up a whole new world for me. I didn't restrict myself to Garbage message boards, for this was not my only interest. I joined many about different bands; I learned what are the best pickups for rock guitar (Seymour Duncans) and I found people with the same interests as me. An offshoot of message boards is chat rooms. I am not a frequent visitor to these; indeed, I have only been in two in my life. These were special occasions when a band would be present in the chat room. I have talked to both Nerve and Snake River Conspiracy. From the chat with Snake River Conspiracy I got a signed photo and a limited-edition CD.

And finally, stage three. My oxygen. Yahoo Instant Messenger. Even typing those delicious words makes me want to log on. Could I? Will I? Yahoo Instant Messenger is, surprisingly, an instant messenger service. This means messages can be sent instantly to other people online and so you can hold conversations. This does not sound extremely amazing, 'Woo-hoo having a conversation, what will people think of next!' Indeed, I cannot explain the wonder of this device. Perhaps it is because I find holding spoken conversations difficult. On the internet I can project me; my insecurities about my looks, the fear of people around me laughing are gone. That is a great feeling. Perhaps it is that great function – the 'ignore' button. Person annoying you? Press ignore, you don't need to get any more messages from them. Maybe it is the fact that you can look at people's profiles; get a bit of background information before jumping into a conversation. Maybe it is that it is easy to find people with the same interests as you – and someone definitely will, the whole world is connected! But actually I think I do know, it is because of the people I talk to. I only know my best friend over the internet; she lives in Birmingham and I've never met her in my life, but she's still my best friend. This is a simplification of my net life; there are other factors, other magnificent things I have found. For instance, the downloading of MP3s, mailing lists … but going into the wonders of the web would take days.

So, in conclusion, yes, I am addicted, I know it. I am a lot happier on the net than in rl (real life, for the uneducated) and I think this is because of the people I talk to. My parents think I am anti-social in spending so much time online, but it is online that I am the most social. It's part of my life now, and I'm glad it is. I must have been really bored before.

Questions

1 How interesting did you find the subject matter?
2 Did the personality of the writer come through?
3 Was there any humour?
4 How was the piece of writing structured?
5 Was there development in the writer's thoughts/feelings?
6 How successfully were narrative, descriptive and reflective elements combined?
7 Which stylistic features were used to good effect? (For example, word choice, sentence structure, imagery, repetition or any other techniques.)

Mark awarded: ____/15

Marker's comment:

IMAGINATIVE WRITING: PROSE FICTION

The other type of writing you might choose from the creative genre is imaginative writing. Imaginative writing may take the form of prose fiction, a drama script or poetry.

What is fiction?

The dictionary definition of fiction is a piece of literature 'concerning imaginary characters and events'. 'Imaginary' is defined as 'existing only in the mind, not real'.

In order to be interesting, however, your story must be close to reality. It is well known that successful authors often base their characters on real people. You may also feature real events – for example, many writers have used the Second World War as a setting.

> At Oxford, Evelyn Waugh hated his history tutor, Mr Cruttwell, who eventually had him expelled from the university. Waugh based several unpleasant, snobbish characters in his novels on him, sometimes even using his name. The title character in 'Mr Loveday's Little Outing', which is about a serial killer, was originally called Cruttwell.

In the Introduction to this book, you were asked to think about what you already know and about the opinions you hold. These ideas should be applied to your fiction as well as to your non-fiction writing.

Form

Prose fiction may take the form of a complete short story, although it will not be as long as most of those published in collections by professional writers. You might also imagine that you are writing a full-length novel, and present your piece of writing in the form of an episode or chapter from it.

Alternatively, you might wish to write a piece of pure description, in order to present a picture in words or to create a mood. Your writing might also take the form of a character sketch, focusing on a single imaginary person. (You could, of course, also describe a real person, although this type of writing would fall into the personal/reflective category.)

A story or episode from a novel will require several elements. Among the most important of these are theme, plot, setting and characters. After you have decided on these, you can then decide on the structure and style you will adopt to make your writing most effective.

Theme

A story should have a clear theme: an underlying idea that is developed through the plot. Your story is likely to be more effective if the theme is something about which you feel strongly. The way your writing reflects your thoughts on the world around you is what will make it original and interesting to the reader.

For practice (1)

On page x of the Introduction you were asked to think about your opinions on various topics.

Question

Look back at the table on that page, then write down the theme(s) contained in each of the statements. The first one has been done for you.

Statement	Themes
a)	The generation gap; social change
b)	
c)	
d)	
e)	
f)	
g)	
h)	
i)	
j)	

For practice (2)

In small groups, hold a brainstorming session. Think of as many other themes as you can, and make a list of these.

Tip

Emotions and feelings can also provide themes for a story.

Plot

The plot is what happens in a story and what the characters do. Many people agree that there are only a few plot patterns, which can be found (with variations) in all books, plays and films.

Boy meets girl	The quest	Entry into a new world	Rags to riches (or the ugly duckling)
A character falls in love with someone who may or may not return these feelings. Obstacles to happiness may or may not be overcome. **Examples**: Shakespeare's *Romeo and Juliet*; the film *West Side Story*; John Wain's 'Mort'; George Mackay Brown's 'Silver'.	A journey in search of treasure or happiness, or to find out the truth. **Examples**: *The Third Man* by Graham Greene; *Lord of the Rings* by J.R.R. Tolkien; the film *Raiders of the Lost Ark*.	Chance brings a character into a strange new world in which challenges and dangers must be overcome. **Examples**: *Robinson Crusoe* by Daniel Defoe; *The Beach* by Alex Garland; *Lord of the Flies* by William Golding.	An ordinary or downtrodden person wins recognition or wealth. **Examples**: *Cinderella*; *Great Expectations* and *Oliver Twist* by Charles Dickens; Audrey Manley Tucker's short story 'Wanted – a Miracle'; the film *My Fair Lady*.

Spider and fly	Nemesis	Overcoming the monster	Tit for tat
An innocent person is lured into a trap. **Examples**: Roald Dahl's 'The Landlady'; *Felicia's Journey* by William Trevor.	A mistake or bad deed has consequences; foolishness is exposed and punished. **Examples**: *Emma* by Jane Austen; *The Mayor of Casterbridge* by Thomas Hardy; *Crime and Punishment* by Fyodor Dostoevsky.	A hero or heroine confronts a monster, and defeats it against the odds. The monster might be metaphorical, such as a bully. A variant is 'David and Goliath', where the victor is much smaller. **Examples**: *Frankenstein* by Mary Shelley; *Dracula* by Bram Stoker; the film *Jaws;* Alexander Reid's 'The Kitten'.	A character achieves a fitting revenge. **Examples**: Saki's 'Sredni Vashtar'; *The Count of Monte Cristo* by Alexandre Dumas.

For practice

Write down the names of any short stories, novels, plays or films you can remember well. Can you assign them to one or more of the basic plot patterns, with a brief explanation?

Example	Plot pattern
The Harry Potter series	Overcoming the monster (Harry is pitched against the evil Voldemort).
Alice in Wonderland	Entry into a strange new world.

Faction

You may decide to write about a real event, rather than inventing a plot. You have to flesh out the facts – what you know happened – by imagining exactly how the people behaved, what they were thinking and what they said to each other. This type of writing is sometimes known as faction.

Such imaginary depictions of real events have frequently been made into films. An example is *Braveheart*, which imagined the life of William Wallace. The scriptwriters had to imagine what the historical figures said and did. This helped bring a slice of history to life.

The novel *Biko* by Donald Woods is an example of 'faction'. It is a fictionalised account of the life and death of Steve Biko, a black South African civil rights activist.

Steve Biko

Setting

The setting is an important element of fiction. This refers to the place and time in which the events in your story are set. If you find thinking up a plot difficult, you might try to get started by creating a setting. This will take the form of a picture in words. You might even find that you produce a good piece of descriptive writing that can stand by itself.

You must make particular choices: In what part of the world will your story be set? What time of day? What will the weather be like? You may have in mind a real place that you know – it is quite in order to describe it exactly, or you may fictionalise it to suit your purposes.

If you wish to recreate a past time, try to imagine details that would belong to the period and make your description convincing.

An effective setting will often do more than just create a picture – it may also set a mood that is appropriate to the story.

For practice (1)

Look at the following extracts from stories that present a setting in time and place and also evoke a particular mood. The questions that follow are designed to draw your attention to techniques that you could try yourself when creating settings.

Beneath the great grey cliff of Clogher Mor there was a massive square black rock, dotted with white limpets, sitting in the sea. The sea rose and fell about it frothing. Rising, the sea hoisted the seaweed that grew along the rock's rims until the long, winding strands spread like streams of blood through the white foam. Falling, the tide sucked the strands down taut from their bulbous roots.

Silence. It was noon. The sea was calm. Rock-birds slept on its surface, their beaks resting on their fat white breasts. Tall seagulls standing on one leg dozed high up in the ledges of the cliff. On the great rock there was a flock of black cormorants resting, bobbing their long necks to draw food from their swollen gullets.

From 'The Wounded Cormorant' by Liam O'Flaherty

Questions

1 Look at the author's use of **colours** in this opening to the story. What associations do these colours have? List them, and suggest what mood is evoked.
2 Pick out words and phrases from the **first** paragraph that suggest the immense power of nature. Try to explain how they do this.
3 Pick out all the words in the **second** paragraph that suggest quiet and stillness.
4 The second paragraph begins with three very short sentences. What effect does this create? Do you feel it matches the ideas of quiet and stillness, or conflicts with them to start creating tension?
5 Consider the phrases 'like streams of blood' and 'draw food from their swollen gullets'. Explain what expectations they might set up in the reader as to how the story will develop.

This extract is from a novel about a young pick-pocket, and is set in the slums of eighteenth-century London.

Between Saffron Hill and Turnmill Street stood – or rather slouched – the Red Lion Tavern. A very evil-looking, tumble-down structure, weather-boarded on three sides and bounded on the fourth by the great Fleet Ditch which stank and gurgled and gurgled and stank by day and night, like the parlour of the Tavern itself.

This parlour was an ill-lit, noxious place. Thieves, pick-pockets, foot-pads, unlucky swindlers and ruined gamblers boozed and snoozed here, and were presided over by a greasy landlord who never sold a customer to the gallows for less than a guinea.

From Smith by Leon Garfield

Questions

1 Pick out the expressions that build up the impression that the Red Lion Tavern is a sinister place.
2 Garfield is a contemporary writer, but he uses a number of old-fashioned words to convey a flavour of the past. Can you pick these out?
3 The writer uses personification in the word 'slouched' (line 1). Explain exactly why this is so effective here.
4 Garfield's setting is full of life, although sinister. What language techniques help create this impression?

The Third Man is *a thriller set just after the end of the Second World War. It is narrated by a British policeman who is investigating black-market crimes.*

I never knew Vienna between the wars … to me it is simply a city of undignified ruins which turned that February into great glaciers of snow and ice. The Danube was a grey flat muddy river a long way off across the Second Bezirk[1], the Russian zone where the Prater[2] lay smashed and desolate and full of weeds, only the Great Wheel revolving slowly over the foundations of merry-go-rounds like abandoned millstones, the rusting iron of smashed tanks which nobody had cleared away, the frost-nipped weeds where the snow was thin. I haven't enough imagination to picture it as it had once been, any more than I can picture Sacher's Hotel[3] as other than a transit hotel for English officers, or see the Kärntnerstrasse as a fashionable shopping street instead of a street which exists, most of it, only at eye level, repaired up to the first storey.

From The Third Man by Graham Greene

[1] Bezirk – district
[2] Prater – amusement park
[3] Sacher's Hotel – formerly a luxury five-star hotel

Questions

1 Pick out all the expressions that suggest destruction, desolation and alienation, contributing to a bleak mood.
2 Pick out the references to the weather. What do they contribute to the mood?
3 What is the effect of the references to happier times? Suggest a reason why the author focuses on an amusement park in presenting the scene.

For practice (2)

Think of a place you know well. Try to imagine it as it would be either a) around a hundred years ago, or b) after a war had changed it.

Write a descriptive paragraph in which you focus on evoking a mood: for example, happiness, liveliness, desolation, dreariness, etc.

Characters

A good story will feature memorable characters who are convincingly real. The mark of a good storyteller is that their characters will touch the reader's heart in some way, arousing emotions such as sympathy or curiosity or dislike. A character may be based on a living person, or even be a composite of several real people.

Show and tell: you can bring your characters to life by telling the readers facts about them, and can also show what they are like by what they say and do.

For practice (1)

The short story 'Mort' by John Wain contains some very effective characterisation. In the following extracts from the story, you will see techniques that you might try yourself when you construct your characters.

The story is narrated by 18-year-old Michael, looking back to events that happened when he was a thoughtless 16-year-old. The main themes of the story are guilt and betrayal, and the plot tells of how Michael lets down a good friend because of his infatuation with a beautiful but worthless girl.

In the first section, Michael both tells and shows the reader what his friend Mort is like, but the writer presents the information in such a way that aspects of Michael's own character emerge in the telling.

In this opening section, the narrator tells the reader some facts about Mort. The main focus is on Mort's vulnerability.

Elizabeth Bennet and Mr Darcy are memorable characters from the Jane Austen novel *Pride and Prejudice*. They have been portrayed in a 1995 BBC adaptation by Jennifer Ehle and Colin Firth (above) and in a 2005 film version by Keira Knightley and Matthew Macfadyen.

> Mort was fourteen. He had this awful disease, I forget the scientific name for it, where your bones are as soft as chalk. If he moved quickly across the room and bumped against the table or something, the kind of knock you or I wouldn't even feel, he broke a bone. Every single time. Sometimes he broke his bones just turning over in bed. He was always having to be plastered up. And remember when Mort broke a bone, though it was so easily done, it *hurt* just as much as if you or I broke one.
>
> Poor old Mort. I used to feel so damn sorry for him. Walking back home from his house, I don't know why I didn't burst out crying sometimes. Why did it have to happen to him, I used to think, why, why, why? He was so gentle. He had nothing but gentleness in him.

Questions

1 List the expressions that clearly convey Mort's vulnerability to the reader.
2 What phrase does Michael use twice to involve the reader?
3 In Michael's narrative, Wain convincingly reproduces the 'voice' of a teenage boy. He uses certain techniques for emphasis. Find an example of each of the following, and explain its particular effect:
   a) short sentence
   b) minor sentence
   c) repetition
   d) italics
   e) any **one** other language technique.
4 Wain conveys something of the character of Michael, the narrator. In the first paragraph Michael expresses great sympathy for Mort, but in the second paragraph his sympathy is revealed to be rather limited.
   a) Describe Michael's tone in 'poor old Mort' and 'so damn sorry'.
   b) What other clues are there to suggest that Michael's sympathy for Mort is not very deep?

For practice (2)

The next development of the story is a piece of dialogue in which the author shows Mort's personality and the relationship between the boys through what they say. Some further aspects of Michael's personality also emerge.

Mort's character emerges in a very positive light, compared with Michael's.

One particular afternoon we'd been watching a football match on his little TV.

'Look, Mort,' I said. I couldn't keep it back. 'When you watch football on TV, how does it make you feel?'

'Feel?' he said. 'I like to watch it if it's a good game, naturally.'

'Yes, but I mean, how does it make you feel in yourself?'

'You mean because I can't play games?' he asked.

'Well, yes, I mean, there are these twenty-two guys, all very fit, rushing up and down the field and slamming the ball around and you … well … doesn't it sort of rub it all in?'

'Oh, sometimes,' said Mort. I could see he wanted to change the subject. 'I mean, you just have to try to keep yourself busy and not think too much about it. It's blind people I'm sorry for.' Then he got his new stamp album out.

'There's hardly anything in it yet,' he said. 'I don't spend any money on it, you see. The way I've got it worked out, photography costs a lot, and my dad's very good about giving me enough money for that, so I try to have one hobby I don't spend anything at all on. Just the hinges.'

Then his face clouded over a bit. 'It's going to take me one hell of a time to get anything in it,' he said. 'With not buying stamps. I just get the ones people give me off their letters. And we don't seem to know anybody abroad. I hardly ever get a foreign one.'

[*Michael decides to help. His father gets a lot of foreign mail, and he finds some stamps from South Korea on an envelope. He phones Mort to tell him the good news.*]

'Your luck's changed,' I said, 'now that you've got me working as your agent. I've got a scoop for you already. Six stamps and guess where from? I'll give you a clue – it's in the East.'

'China?' he said. 'Japan?'

'South Korea,' I said. I knew he'd go straight and find it, on his globe. 'The Republic of South Korea.'

'Magic,' Mort breathed down the telephone. 'When can I have them?'

'I'll drop by,' I said.

Questions

1 What evidence is there in the dialogue of the following aspects of Mort's personality?
   a) lack of self-pity
   b) dislike of being an **object** of pity
   c) a very positive attitude to life, despite his disability
   d) maturity and consideration of others.
2 What evidence is there that Michael is:
   a) tactless
   b) impulsive
   c) full of himself
   d) self-centred?

Before he can 'drop by' to give Mort the stamps, Michael becomes infatuated with Fiona, the beautiful daughter of one of his father's colleagues. He takes her to his school disco, where she allows him to kiss her. When he learns that Fiona 'collects' things he gives her the South Korean stamps. However, Fiona later admits to Michael that she only accepted the stamps in the hope of selling them because she wanted money to buy clothes. She carelessly left them in a pocket and the stamps were ruined when they were put through the wash.

For practice (3)

Wain's story ends with a short epilogue in which Michael visits Mort in order to confess that he cannot give him the stamps after all. The calm, mature way in which Mort copes with his disappointment provides a very poignant ending. The writer also shows, without telling us directly, that Michael has matured.

The next afternoon I went round to see Mort. I reckoned I might as well get it over. His mother told me he was in his room so I went straight up. What she didn't tell me was that he had broken another bone. His left forearm was plastered up and in a sling.

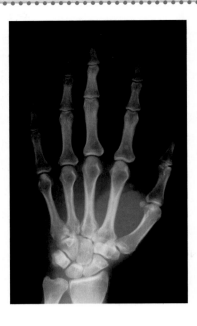

'I did it just yesterday,' he told me.

'I'm really sorry, Mort.'

'Oh, it isn't so serious,' he said. 'Just a small bone in my wrist. It doesn't hurt much. Did you see that ice hockey on TV last night? Those two Canadian teams?'

'No,' I said.

'Sensational,' he said. 'The body-checking … wow!'

'Ice hockey's quite a game,' I said. 'Look, Mort. I've got some bad news.'

'It's about the stamps, isn't it?' he said.

'How d'you know?'

'Because you haven't given them to me yet,' he said. 'If you were going to, it would have been the first thing you mentioned. You'd have had them in your hand as you came through the door because you're like that.'

'Well, look, Mort, you might as well know, the stamps got destroyed,' I said. That much at least was true, now for the lies. 'I didn't cut them off the envelope, I thought you might have fun doing that, and I left the envelope on the work table in my room. It was lying with a bunch of old envelopes and our cleaning woman picked the whole lot up and threw them away.'

We have no cleaning woman. We clean the house ourselves, when we get round to it.

'Where did she throw them to?' Mort asked.

'She burnt them. She always burns the waste paper in the garden incinerator. She ought to send it to be recycled but she never does.'

'Well,' Mort said, 'it would have been a waste to recycle Korean stamps. I'd rather think of them being burnt, somehow.'

'I'm sorry, Mort,' I said.

'It's not your fault,' he said. His stamp album, I now saw, was open on the table and I would have taken a bet, although I didn't look, that it was open at K. 'It was nice of you anyway.'

'What was nice of me?'

'To want to give me the stamps,' he said.

I was silent, then said, 'I hope your wrist doesn't hurt too much.'

'Oh, not too much,' he said. 'It aches but I'll get used to it.'

Questions

1   Michael goes to see Mort 'the next afternoon'. How does this contrast with his earlier attitude, and what change in Michael does this indicate?
2   Compare Michael's expressions of sympathy and his comment on the ice hockey game with those he made in the first two extracts.
3   Michael lies to Mort about the true fate of the stamps. The writer leaves it to the reader to decide if Michael is right or wrong to do this. What do you think?
4   What other details combine to make the ending moving for the reader?

Memo

Note the techniques used by John Wain in this story to create his characters:

*   Using straightforward, factual description.
*   Using direct speech, which allows the characters to emerge through what they say.
*   Allowing the reader to draw their own conclusions from what the characters say and do.

Interaction

Wain presents a convincing relationship between Michael and Mort. By adding Fiona, Wain has created a triangle of characters – three is a good number of characters for a short story. The third character drives the plot and affects the relationship of the other two.

For practice

Devise a group of three teenage characters. Give them names, and write descriptions of them. Don't forget things like height, eye colour and the clothes they wear. You can even decide whether they have any annoying habits, like playing with their hair or chewing their pencil. Try to make them as lifelike as possible. You might look for photographs in a magazine or on the internet showing how you picture them.

Exchange your ideas with a partner or within a group, and discuss the effect that your characters have on the readers. You can then decide if you wish to develop your ideas into a complete story.

Symbolism

Finally, think about this sentence:

> They were just stiff crumpled bits of paper at the end of it so I threw them away.

This is how Fiona describes the fate of the South Korean stamps.

Sometimes, a writer introduces an image that clearly represents something deeper. This is known as symbolism.

This negative image might represent several ideas: the death of Michael's hopes of a relationship with Fiona; Michael's promise to Mort; Mort's disappointment.

In the short story 'Silver' by George Mackay Brown, a young fisherman takes three fish to a girl he is visiting. The boy gives away two fish in return for information about the girl, while his last fish is reduced to 'a jagged skeleton' by some cats while he is talking to the girl's sister. This vivid image represents the end of the love affair.

When you write a short story, think of a suitable image that you could use as a symbol to suggest a theme.

Structure

You have decided on a theme, created a setting in time and place, devised a number of characters and selected a basic plot. You must now choose how you will present your story.

Point of view

The point of view of the narrative is an important choice. You may provide an impersonal overview by means of a third-person account of events, referring to your characters by their names or as 'he', 'she', 'they' and so on. This is called an omniscient (or 'all-knowing') narrative stance. Such a method allows you to explain what each character is thinking. Most writers, however, prefer to present the events from one character's point of view (although other people's views will often emerge). For example, in the short story 'Mort' (see pages 21–24), the point of view is Michael's. The reader, however, can also infer what Mort is thinking from what he says and does.

'Mort' is narrated in the first person, and John Wain successfully reproduces the 'voice' of a thoughtless and sometimes rude and awkward teenager. Look at the following extract:

> The next morning, at breakfast, I got on to my old man.
>
> 'I'm collecting stamps, Dad,' I said. 'For Mort.'
>
> 'Postage stamps?' he said keenly. Scientists have to get things right. I suppose he thought there was a possibility Mort might have been collecting trading stamps or excise stamps.
>
> 'If you look at a letter,' I said, indicating the little pile of same by his place at the table, 'you'll see that in the right-hand top corner there's a piece of coloured paper, stuck on, with a numeral on it. That's a stamp. Mort collects them.'
>
> 'Don't be so rude to your father, Michael,' said my mother.
>
> 'Oh, he's not being rude,' said my father. 'Just sarcastic. Everybody's sarcastic at that age. I was myself.'

In this extract, John Wain successfully recreates the exaggerated sarcasm typical of an arrogant teenager.

Question

Look carefully at the word choice and tone in the extract above. How does Wain show that Michael's sarcasm is ridiculously overdone? Explain how Wain makes the scene both comic and believable.

In 'Mort', the narrative is in the first person. Michael refers to himself as 'I', and the reader has the impression that Michael is there, telling us what happened.

A single point of view can be presented equally well in the third person, however. The writer tells us what a character thinks and feels, and presents the other characters as this particular character sees them.

For practice (1)

Look at the opening of this short story, 'The Kitten' by Alexander Reid, and then answer the questions that follow.

The feet were tramping directly towards her. In the hot darkness under the tarpaulin the cat cuffed a kitten to silence and listened intently.

She could hear the scruffling and scratching of hens about the straw-littered yard; the muffled grumbling of the turning churn in the dairy; the faint clink and jangle of harness from the stable – drowsy, comfortable, reassuring noises through which the clang of the iron-shod boots on the cobbles broke ominously.

The boots ground to a halt, and three holes in the cover, brilliant diamond-points of light, went suddenly black. Crouching, the cat waited, then sneezed and drew back as the tarpaulin was thrown up and glaring white sunlight struck at her eyes.

She stood over her kittens, the fur of her back bristling and the pupils of her eyes narrowed to pin-points. A kitten mewed plaintively.

For a moment, the hired man stared stupidly at his discovery, then turned towards the stable and called harshly: 'Hi, Maister! Here a wee.'

A second pair of boots clattered across the yard, and the face of the farmer, elderly, dark and taciturn, turned down on the cats.

'So that's whaur she's been,' commented the newcomer slowly.

Although the story is told by an omniscient narrator, the point of view is that of a mother cat, who has given birth to her kittens behind a tarpaulin in the farmyard.

Questions

1 What expressions does the author use to describe the humans to show that they are very much bigger than the cat?
2 It is dark under the tarpaulin. Which figures of speech does the author use to indicate that the cat's dominant sense is her hearing?
3 Compare the way the animal noises are described with the way the human sounds are presented. How does the author suggest that the other animals are not threatening or frightening to the cat, while the humans are?
4 Show how the author makes the reader aware of the cat's ultra-sensitive eyesight.

For practice (2)

- Write a few paragraphs from the point of view of an animal encountering a person. Think about the size and special characteristics of the animal, and how the human world must appear to it.

- Compare your writing with a partner or within a group, and assess how successful you have been in capturing the spirit of the animal.

- With your partner, group or teacher, discuss whether your writing could be successfully developed into a full-length piece.

It is also possible to alternate between two or more different points of view. For example, a family event such as a wedding or a funeral could be fascinating if different views were expressed on it.

Ordering events

You must also decide how to present the events of your plot to the greatest advantage.

The simplest way to present the events is in the order in which they happen: this is known as a linear structure.

It might be more interesting, however, to start in the middle or at the end of a series of events. The reader will at once be intrigued about how the action reached this point and wish to read further. This technique is called flashback.

'The Vertical Ladder' by William Sansom is a good example of flashback structure. The opening paragraph begins at a point near the end of the action. A young man called Flegg is climbing an enormous gasometer by means of a vertical ladder that runs up the outside of it. As he climbs, he starts to suffer from severe vertigo (dizziness caused by heights).

> As he felt the first watery eggs of sweat moistening the palms of his hands, as with every rung higher his body seemed to weigh more heavily, this young man Flegg regretted in sudden desperation but still in vain, the irresponsible events that had thrust him up into his present precarious climb. Here he was, isolated on a vertical iron ladder flat to the side of a gasometer and bound to climb higher and higher until he should reach the summit.
>
> *From 'The Vertical Ladder' by William Sansom*

Questions

1 What emotion does the author evoke in the first sentence?
2 The reader is forced to imagine what 'irresponsible events' could lead a young man to make such a dangerous climb. What reason might there be?
3 The reader then wonders what will happen next. Will he fall? Will he make it to the top? Will the story end in anticlimax as he just climbs down? What do you think would make the most successful ending to this story?

Sansom continues his story with a flashback to explain how Flegg got into this situation, and the rest of the story follows his ascent of the vertical ladder.

Openings

Structurally, the opening of your story is very important. It must act as a hook to engage the reader. In the case of 'The Vertical Ladder', the reader is drawn in at once to the plight of the character and reads on to find out how the situation develops.

For practice (1)

Look at the following extract, which is the opening to 'Silver' by George Mackay Brown. The narrator of the story is a young fisherman, whom we are told later is just seventeen years old.

In these few lines, Mackay Brown makes clear his themes, and also gives intriguing hints as to character and plot.

'You'll never get her,' said the skipper of the *Kestrel*. 'She's meant for some rich farmer on the hill.' He shook his head.

The three other fishermen of the *Kestrel* shook their heads. 'You're too poor,' they said.

Bert the cook laughed sarcastically.

I took the three best haddocks I could find from the morning's catch and set out for the farm.

They shook their heads after me.
The skipper took his pipe from his mouth and spat – he thought I must have gone out of my mind.

Questions

1   What themes are suggested in the first few sentences?
2   Ignoring all the discouragement, the narrator just selects the 'best' fish and sets off for the farm where the girl of his dreams lives. What does this tell us about his character? How does the reader react to his response to the mockery?
3   How would you imagine the plot developing? (Think about: 'She's meant for some rich farmer' and 'You're too poor'.)

For practice (2)

Here is a selection of openings from short stories and novels by well-known authors.

In pairs or small groups, discuss how effective these openings are. You could consider aspects such as:

• What kind of atmosphere is created?

• What clues are given about the story to follow?

• What makes the reader want to read on?

• How are techniques such as word choice and punctuation used to create a particular effect?

1 They were going to get me. I saw them the moment I turned the corner. They were halfway down, waiting near the bus stop. Melanie, Sarah and Kim. Kim, the worst one of all. (Jacqueline Wilson, *Bad Girls*)

2 There is an old house in Kent not far from the sea where a little ghost girl plays in the garden. (Jane Gardam, 'Bang, Bang – Who's Dead?')

3 My mother was twice married. She never spoke of her first husband, and it is only from other people that I have learnt what little I know of him. (Elizabeth Gaskell, 'The Half-Brothers')

4 A middle-aged man wearing a dirty raincoat, who badly needed a shave and looked as though he hadn't washed for a month, came out of a public lavatory with a cloth bag of tools folded beneath his arm. Standing for a moment on the edge of the pavement to adjust his cap – the cleanest thing about him – he looked casually to left and right and, when the flow of traffic had eased off, crossed the road. (Alan Sillitoe, 'Uncle Ernest')

5 Connie began to have the feeling of dread and uneasiness in the taxi but told herself it was not reasonable. (Will F. Jenkins, 'Uneasy Homecoming')

6 For four hours every morning, and for twenty minutes before a large audience at night, Fletcher was locked up with murder. (Phyllis Bottome, 'Henry')

7 True! – nervous – very, very dreadfully nervous I had been and am; but why will you say that I am mad? (Edgar Allan Poe, 'The Tell-Tale Heart')

8 When Chas awakened, the air-raid shelter was silent. Grey winter light was creeping round the door curtain. It could have been anytime. (Robert Westall, *The Machine Gunners*)

9 My earliest memories are a confusion of hilly fields and dark, deep stables and rats that scampered along the beams above my head. But I remember well enough the day of the horse-sale. The terror of it stayed with me all my life. I was not yet six months old, a gangling, leggy colt who had never been further than a few feet from his mother. (Michael Morpurgo, *War Horse*)

10 During the whole of a dull, dark and soundless day in the autumn of the year, when the clouds hung oppressively low in the heavens, I had been passing alone, on horseback, through a singularly dreary tract of country, and at length found myself, as the shades of evening drew on, within view of the melancholy House of Usher. (Edgar Allan Poe, 'The Fall of the House of Usher')

Endings

Many people find it difficult to know how to end a story. A useful piece of advice is to start by devising the end. You can then structure your story to lead up to this ending. Such a technique almost always leads to a satisfactory story.

An ending need not be conclusive – often the most interesting stories leave the reader to do some thinking.

Of the two stories examined on pages 28 and 29, 'Silver' has a clear outcome. The young fisherman arrives at the farm to be told by the girl's sister that she has left home to marry someone richer. While he is talking, the farm cats devour his fish. The reader feels sympathy for the boy, but we are left in no doubt as to the fate of his first love affair.

In 'The Vertical Ladder', however, the protagonist is left stranded near the top of the gasometer. He cannot reach the top because the last few rungs of the ladder are missing, but he cannot descend because he has become paralysed with fear. The reader is left wondering how he will be rescued from this stranded position – a disturbing picture.

A twist is an unexpected ending. A famous example occurs in 'The Necklace', by the French writer Guy de Maupassant.

A pretty young woman, Mme Loisel, borrows a beautiful diamond necklace from a friend, Mme Forestier, to wear to a party, but on returning home discovers she has lost it. Too proud to admit this, she borrows a huge sum of money and buys an identical necklace to give back in its place. Her life is virtually ruined as she has to work very hard and live in poverty for ten years in order to pay back the loan. Mme Loisel loses her beauty in the struggle for survival.

This is how the story ends:

One Sunday, when she had gone for a stroll in the Champs Elysées as a change from the week's grind, she suddenly saw a lady taking a child for a walk. It was Mme Forestier, still young, still beautiful, still attractive.

Mme Loisel felt a wave of emotion. Should she speak to her? Yes, she would. Now that she had paid, she would tell her everything. Why not?

She went up to her: 'Good morning, Jeanne!'

The other woman did not recognise her, and surprised at being addressed in this familiar fashion by a common woman; she stammered: 'But Madame … I don't know you … there must be some mistake.'

'No! I'm Mathilde Loisel!'

Her friend exclaimed: 'Oh! Poor Mathilde, how you've changed!'

'Yes, I've had a grim time since I saw you last, with lots of trouble – and it was all your fault!'

'My fault? What do you mean?'

'You remember that diamond necklace you lent me to go to the party at the Ministry?'

'Yes, what about it?'

'Well! I lost it!'

'What! But you brought it back to me.'

'I brought you back another exactly like it; and for ten years we've been paying for it. You'll realise it hasn't been easy, for we had no money of our own. Well, now it's all over and I'm very glad.'

Mme Forestier had stopped: 'You say you bought a diamond necklace to replace mine?'

'Yes! And you never spotted it, did you? They were as like as two peas.' And she smiled with simple proud pleasure.

Mme Forestier, deeply moved, took both her hands: 'Oh, my poor Mathilde! But mine was only paste, not worth more than five hundred francs at most!'

Questions

1 Discuss how effective you find this ending.
2 Suggest alternative endings that the writer might have chosen.

For practice

Devise and write just the ending of a story. Include two or three characters, and provide an outcome of some kind. You should aim to write around 250 words.

- Exchange your ending with that of a partner, or someone in your group.
- Discuss how effective you think they each are.
- Then compile a plan of how the story might develop up to the point of your ending.

Dos and don'ts of effective fiction writing

Do	Don't
Plan how your story will end, and then work up to it.	Embark on a story with no idea how it will end.
Use direct speech sparingly, and in a way that brings out features of the characters.	Use too much direct speech – it will slow up your story.
Write notes on your characters before you begin the plot, so that you 'know' them.	Include too many characters – between one and three is about right for the length of story at which you are aiming.
Think carefully about your settings, and present them with a few vivid details.	Devise an overly complex plot.
Try using a dialect you know well for direct speech.	Resolve your plot by making it all a dream.
Vary your sentence structures.	Use repetitive sentence structures, such as beginning a series of sentences with 'I'.
Be aware of your paragraphing. Try using techniques such as single-sentence paragraphs to build suspense.	Make all your paragraphs too long or too short.

Working with sentence structures

In this extract from 'Uneasy Homecoming' by Will F. Jenkins, different sentence lengths and structures are used to create suspense.

The story tells how a woman called Connie has returned home alone after being on holiday, only to discover that her house has been burgled.

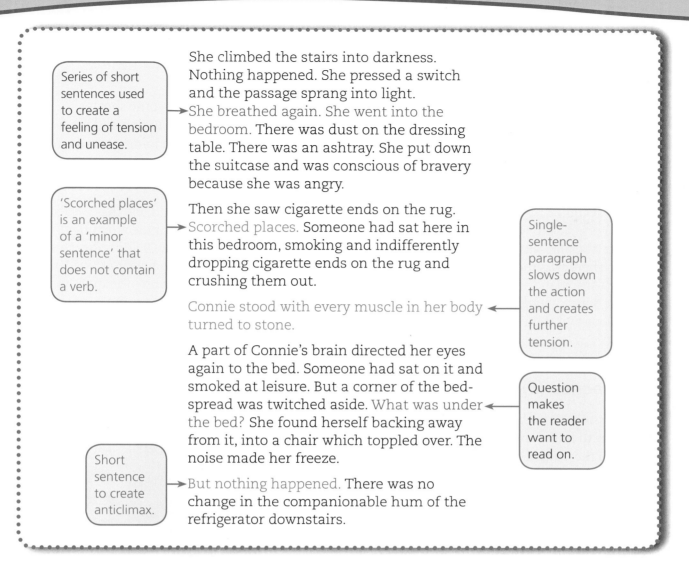

Series of short sentences used to create a feeling of tension and unease.

'Scorched places' is an example of a 'minor sentence' that does not contain a verb.

Short sentence to create anticlimax.

Single-sentence paragraph slows down the action and creates further tension.

Question makes the reader want to read on.

She climbed the stairs into darkness. Nothing happened. She pressed a switch and the passage sprang into light. She breathed again. She went into the bedroom. There was dust on the dressing table. There was an ashtray. She put down the suitcase and was conscious of bravery because she was angry.

Then she saw cigarette ends on the rug. Scorched places. Someone had sat here in this bedroom, smoking and indifferently dropping cigarette ends on the rug and crushing them out.

Connie stood with every muscle in her body turned to stone.

A part of Connie's brain directed her eyes again to the bed. Someone had sat on it and smoked at leisure. But a corner of the bed-spread was twitched aside. What was under the bed? She found herself backing away from it, into a chair which toppled over. The noise made her freeze.

But nothing happened. There was no change in the companionable hum of the refrigerator downstairs.

For practice (1)

Here's how the story continues. Discuss with a partner how sentence patterns are used for different effects.

If one of Them – the nameless Things of which she was in terror now – was under the bed, he would come out at the noise.

Presently – her breathing loud in her own ears – Connie bent and looked under the bed. She had to. None of Them was under it. Of course. But there was an object there which was strange.

A very long time later, Connie dragged it out. It was a bag with bulges in it. Her hands shook horribly, but she dumped its contents on the floor. There were cameras. Silver. Sally Hamilton's necklace and rings. There were watches and fountain pens. This must be what the burglars had taken from the Hamiltons' house and the Blairs' and the Smithsons' and the Tourneys'. The cameras and pens and watches came from Saddlers' shop, where Mr Field had come upon the burglars and they had beaten him almost to death. The burglars had nearly killed him.

For practice (2)

The following extract from the story has been altered so that the sentences simply run into each other with no change of pace and no suspense.

Rewrite them using the techniques we have been exploring, so that you create some shorter sentences to make the narrative more dramatic. The punctuation will need changing and you will have to make minor alterations to the wording, such as taking out some of the joining words. You should also divide the passage into two or three paragraphs.

> They would know she had darkened the house to hide in it so that she could use the telephone. There was a soft sound at the back door and it squeaked and Connie stood rigid as the clicking of the dial would tell everything and she could not conceivably summon help. There was the soft whisper of a foot on the kitchen floor and Connie's hands closed convulsively and the one thought that came to her now was that she must breathe quietly. There was a grey glow somewhere as the figure in the kitchen was throwing a torch beam on the floor and then it halted as he knew that she was hiding somewhere in the house.

For practice (3)

Doris Lessing is another writer who uses varied sentence structures to build up suspense. Her well known story 'Through the Tunnel' tells of a boy called Jerry who sets himself the challenge of swimming through an underwater tunnel. In this extract, he is in the final stages of his swim.

List the ways in which Lessing varies her sentence structures and lengths in order to increase suspense and build up to a climax.

> A hundred, a hundred and one… The water paled. Victory filled him. His lungs were beginning to hurt. A few more strokes and he would be out. He was counting wildly; he said a hundred and fifteen, and then, a long time later, a hundred and fifteen again. The water was a clear jewel-green all around him. Then he saw, above his head, a crack running up through the rock. Sunlight was falling through it, showing the clean dark rock of the tunnel, a single mussel shell, and darkness ahead.
>
> He was at the end of what he could do. He looked up at the crack as if it were filled with air and not water, as if he could put his mouth to it to draw in air. A hundred and fifteen, he heard himself say inside his head – but he had said that long ago. He must go on into the blackness ahead, or he would drown. His head was swelling, his lungs cracking. A hundred and fifteen, a hundred and fifteen pounded through his head, and he feebly clutched at rocks in the dark, pulling himself forward, leaving the brief space of sunlit water behind. He felt he was dying. He was no longer quite conscious. He struggled on in the darkness between lapses into unconsciousness. An immense, swelling pain filled his head, and then the darkness cracked with an explosion of green light. His hands, groping forward, met nothing, and his feet, kicking back, propelled him out into the open sea.

In the extracts looked at so far, you will have seen a number of different techniques that can be used to produce more interesting sentence patterns:

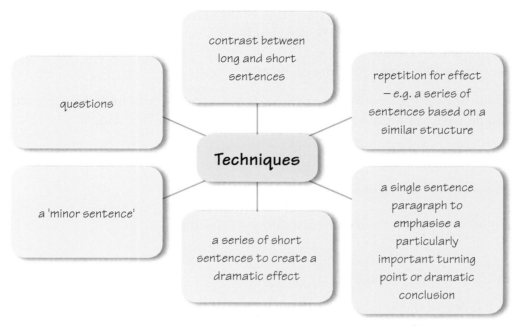

Here is another exercise in which you can practise using these methods.

For practice (4)

In this extract from a student's essay, there is almost no variety of pace. Rewrite the passage using several of the techniques listed above in order to transform this from a dull piece of writing into something more readable. (Again, minor alterations to wording such as removing joining words will be necessary.)

> Before I started at my new school I spent every night worrying about what it would be like. I couldn't stop thinking of how people would react to me. I wondered if they would like me. I wondered what would happen if I didn't make any new friends. I was also anxious that I would lose the friends I already had. Then the day I had been dreading eventually arrived but everything was completely different from what I had imagined and I discovered that my predicament was shared by most of the other students and I immediately regretted worrying myself sick over nothing. I learnt that fear of the unknown can be such a destructive force.

Warning!

Varied sentence techniques can be misused, or overused. Here's someone who has overdone the 'minor sentence' technique:

> Day after day, imagining what changing school would be like. Days passing. Losing your friends. Teachers you don't know. Different people. Waiting. Counting off the days on the calendar. A new start.

Most of these 'sentences' are not proper sentences in that they do not contain the basic grammatical requirements of a sentence:

1   A subject (the person or thing doing the action of the verb).
2   A completed form of a verb (a word of doing or being); verbs ending in 'ing' are present participles rather than complete verbs.
3   A statement that makes sense standing on its own.

Therefore, 'Counting off the days on the calendar' is not a sentence. To fulfil the three requirements above, you would have to supply a subject and complete the verb. For example:

> **I was** counting off the days on the calendar.

Incomplete 'minor' sentences should be used only very sparingly.

The advice of a master

George Orwell is one of the finest writers in the English language. In his essay 'Politics and the English Language', he suggests some rules that aspiring writers should follow.

He suggests that the 'scrupulous' writer, in every sentence that he writes, will ask himself at least four questions:

• What am I trying to say?

• What words will express it?

• What image or idiom will make it clearer?

• Is this image fresh enough to have an effect?

And then he should ask himself two more:

• Could I put it more shortly?

• Have I said anything that is avoidably ugly?

Orwell also suggests following these six 'rules':

1   Never use a metaphor, simile or other figure of speech which you are used to seeing in print.
2   Never use a long word where a short one will do.
3   If it is possible to cut a word out, always cut it out.
4   Never use the passive where you can use the active.
5   Never use a foreign phrase, a scientific word or a jargon word if you can think of an everyday English equivalent.
6   Break any of these rules sooner than say anything outright barbarous.

IMAGINATIVE WRITING: DRAMA

The second option for imaginative writing is to produce a drama script. The aim is to entertain and provoke thought in the audience.

The word 'audience' literally means listeners, and although plays may be watched as well as listened to, it is recommended that you focus on the language of drama rather than on its visual aspects – because your script will be a test of writing.

You may write a complete, short, one-act play, or you can imagine you are writing a whole play and produce a scene from it. You might also consider producing a monologue (a dramatic piece for one voice). As in the case of fiction, you must choose a theme, and then devise a plot, a setting and characters.

Is a drama script a good option?

Writing a drama script is not the easiest option, but you may find you have a flair for it. If you are uncertain about producing a full drama script, a monologue could be a good choice.

Read Alan Bennett's *Talking Heads* for an excellent model. His monologues bring out particular aspects of his characters' personalities, such as loneliness or self-delusion, which audiences find very touching.

The Greek philosopher Aristotle believed that drama should follow the three unities of plot, setting and time. This meant that there should be a single plot thread, and the whole drama should take place in a single location and during a single time span. While many successful playwrights, including Shakespeare, have not always kept to these 'rules', Aristotle's advice is worth following when first embarking on drama writing.

The drama of real life

You do not have to invent a plot; many great dramas have been based on true events. For example, Arthur Miller's powerful play *The Crucible* takes as its plot the seventeenth-century witch trials that actually took place in Salem, Massachusetts. However, Miller's underlying aim was to expose the contemporary 'witch trials' taking place in 1950s America – a time when many prominent Americans were put on trial for so-called 'un-American activities' and accused of being communists. Therefore, his theme was persecution. Courtroom scenes make good drama, as Shakespeare demonstrated in *The Merchant of Venice*.

Approaches to drama writing

Some professional playwrights and scriptwriters begin by writing down their ideas in the form of prose. A famous example of this is Graham Greene's *The Third Man*. Greene wrote the book simply as a step towards producing a film script. The film was a major success, but the novel, too, is now regarded as a classic.

In the foreword to the novel, Greene explains how his project began:

> Years back, on the flap of an envelope I had written an opening paragraph:
>
> 'I had paid my last farewell to Harry a week ago, when his coffin was lowered into the frozen February ground, so that it was with incredulity that I saw him pass by, without a sign of recognition, among the host of strangers in the Strand.'

This one sentence contains the germs of plot, setting, characterisation, themes and narrative method. It even hints at the mood of the book. Can you identify each of these elements? Fill in the remaining boxes in the table.

Theme	Mistaken identity; betrayal by a friend.
Setting (weather)	
Characterisation	
Plot	
Narrative method	
Mood (think of images such as 'frozen February' and 'host of strangers')	

The only detail that Greene later changed was the location, which was moved from London to Vienna.

Having written his novella, Greene then adapted it into the form of a film script. Although in his case a full-length feature film was the result, you could use the same approach to produce a short dramatised scene.

Stage directions

Stage directions are the parts of a drama script that are not intended to be spoken, but instead give information to the people performing or presenting the drama. Because your drama script will be read for the purposes of assessment, it is important that your stage directions are in clear, accurate, continuous prose.

> *(Exit, pursued by a bear)*
>
> *A famous stage direction from Shakespeare's* A Winter's Tale

Although some playwrights give very long, detailed stage directions, this would not be advisable when the total length of your piece must not exceed 1,300 words.

The convention is that stage directions are printed in *italics* and placed in brackets, so that they are not confused with the words to be spoken.

Setting

You must choose where your drama is to take place. It is usual to write a short description of this in your opening stage directions.

Settings can make a significant contribution to the theme or mood of a drama, as well as providing a backdrop.

For example, Arthur Miller set *All My Sons* in the backyard (or garden) of an American house. The plot of the drama, which is set just after the Second World War, involves a family secret: the father of the family has lied about his part in providing faulty parts for aeroplane engines that caused air force planes to crash, killing the pilots. Their younger son, a pilot, did not return from the war.

Miller's opening stage directions include the following:

> *The stage is hedged on right and left by tall, closely planted poplars which lend the yard a secluded atmosphere … At the right, beside the house, the entrance of the driveway can be seen, but the poplars cut off view of its continuation downstage. In the left corner, downstage, stands the four-foot-high stump of a slender apple tree whose upper trunk and branches lie toppled beside it, fruit still clinging to its branches.*

Think about the setting

- Why do you think a garden surrounded by a tall, thick hedge is appropriate for this plot?

- What is significant about the fact that the end of the driveway is not visible to the audience?

- What might the broken apple tree represent?

R.C. Sheriff set his First World War drama *Journey's End* in a 'dug-out' – a primitive, underground living area in the front-line trenches. The play ends with all the British characters apparently being overwhelmed in a huge German bombardment.

Sheriff ended his play with a direction that the stage set should collapse, too:

> *A solitary candle burns with a steady flame. The whine of a shell rises to a shriek and bursts on the dug-out roof. The shock stabs out the candle-flame; the timber props of the door cave slowly in, sandbags fall and block the passage to the open air.*

Extremely dramatic when performed, this piece of writing is also very moving when read. Which details are particularly effective and symbolic?

Characters

The advice on characterisation in prose fiction is also relevant when creating characters for a short drama script:

- Focus on and develop a few characters only.

- Allow the nature of your characters to emerge through what they say and do.

- Avoid having a 'narrator' – this is a lazy way to present events. You should aim to progress the action through dialogue, aided by stage directions.

Some playwrights describe their characters in great detail in the stage directions. This is entertaining to read, although it may present a challenge to actors and directors! For the purposes of your English portfolio writing, it would be quite in order for you to do this.

For practice

Look at the following stage directions from George Bernard Shaw's comedy *Androcles and the Lion*, which present the characters of Androcles and his wife for the first time.

> *Androcles and his wife Megaera come along the path. He is a small, thin, ridiculous little man who might be any age from thirty to fifty-five. He has sandy hair, watery compassionate blue eyes, sensitive nostrils and a very presentable forehead; but his good points go no further: his arms and legs and back, though wiry of their kind, look shrivelled and starved. He carries a big bundle, is very poorly clad, and seems tired and hungry.*
>
> *His wife is a rather handsome, pampered slattern, well fed and in the prime of life. She has nothing to carry.*

Questions

1 What details suggest that the audience will sympathise with Androcles?
2 What details suggest that Megaera will be a character the audience will dislike?
3 Which of Shaw's detailed instructions would be most difficult for the director/actors to fulfil? Why do you think Shaw has included them?

Presentation and layout

There are conventions that you must follow in laying out a drama script. These are illustrated in this extract from *All My Sons*:

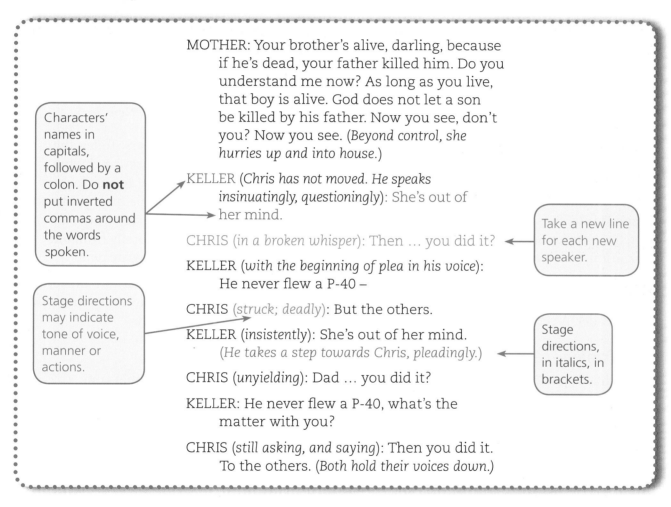

Characters' names in capitals, followed by a colon. Do **not** put inverted commas around the words spoken.

Stage directions may indicate tone of voice, manner or actions.

Take a new line for each new speaker.

Stage directions, in italics, in brackets.

MOTHER: Your brother's alive, darling, because if he's dead, your father killed him. Do you understand me now? As long as you live, that boy is alive. God does not let a son be killed by his father. Now you see, don't you? Now you see. (*Beyond control, she hurries up and into house.*)

KELLER (*Chris has not moved. He speaks insinuatingly, questioningly*): She's out of her mind.

CHRIS (*in a broken whisper*): Then … you did it?

KELLER (*with the beginning of plea in his voice*): He never flew a P-40 –

CHRIS (*struck; deadly*): But the others.

KELLER (*insistently*): She's out of her mind.
    (*He takes a step towards Chris, pleadingly.*)

CHRIS (*unyielding*): Dad … you did it?

KELLER: He never flew a P-40, what's the matter with you?

CHRIS (*still asking, and saying*): Then you did it. To the others. (*Both hold their voices down.*)

IMAGINATIVE WRITING: POETRY

Your piece of imaginative writing may take the form of a poem, or a series of thematically linked poems.

What is poetry?

> The poet Samuel Taylor Coleridge defined poetry as 'the best words in the best order'.

Poet's Walk in Central Park, New York

The question of what poetry actually is has absorbed thinkers for hundreds of years. Today, the first feature people usually think of is rhyme, but many poems do not rhyme. A regular rhythm is another common expectation, but not all poems have regular metres. Particular forms, such as sonnets, are identified easily as poems, but poetry can be quite loose in form; while most poems are arranged into lines, there are exceptions. In ancient times, verse was often the literary form chosen for telling stories because it could be remembered more easily and passed down orally from one generation to another. This is no longer necessary, so why do people continue to write poetry?

Focusing on the beauty of language, as much as on the meaning, is one aspect. Today, we expect poems to express heightened emotions or feelings rather than to tell stories, and to evoke the senses of the reader. A certain intensity of language and thought is common to all poetry.

Caution!

If you choose poetry as your option for the creative section, you should be aware that your submission will not be marked by a regular marker, but it will be referred automatically to the Principal Examiner. Assessing poetry in the context of an examination is difficult for several reasons. The usual rules regarding length do not apply – the only stipulation is that the length is 'appropriate'. Therefore, the examiner might have to decide whether a fairly short poem deserves as good a mark as a story that complies with the stipulated word count. Very few candidates choose the poetry option, and so there are relatively few other examples with which the examiner can compare a candidate's work. Poetry is often profoundly personal, and thus its merits are hard to assess. Even if you are a gifted writer, you will be taking a gamble if you submit a poem as evidence of your talent.

You should probably avoid the poetry option unless:

- You feel you are a committed poet and have already produced a portfolio of poetry.

- The poetry you have already written has attracted praise from your teachers.

- You read and enjoy poetry in general and have a good knowledge of the work and techniques of other poets.

Form

Many modern poets write in free verse, which does not rhyme or have a regular metre. This may seem like an easy option, but taking an easy option may not be the best course for an examination submission. The great American poet Robert Frost described writing free verse as being 'like playing tennis with the net down'. It might be better to aim at achieving some of the recognised technical features of verse, such as following a set metre and organising your poem into regular stanzas. If you can rise to the technical demands of a specific form such as a sonnet, you may gain credit. A sonnet is by definition only fourteen lines long, and so it would be advisable to write a series of thematically linked sonnets in order to achieve the necessary length and depth to gain a good mark.

Language

An awareness of language and the ability to manipulate it in a way that will move and delight the reader is of paramount importance. Striking imagery (fresh, well-chosen similes and metaphors) will enable you to achieve this. Your word choice should also be influenced by a sensitive awareness of how words sound, with the use of techniques such as alliteration and assonance. A sense of pattern in how you arrange your words and structure your sentences – for example, with the use of repetition – will also be effective.

For practice

This poem was written around a hundred years ago by an American poet, Edna St Vincent Millay. Look at the techniques she has used; you might consider attempting some of these in your own poetry.

Sonnet

What lips my lips have kissed, and where, and why
I have forgotten, and what arms have lain
Under my head till morning, but the rain
Is full of ghosts tonight, that tap and sigh
5   Upon the glass and listen for reply,
And in my heart there stirs a quiet pain
For unremembered lads that not again
Will turn to me at midnight with a cry.

Thus in winter stands a lonely tree,
10   Nor knows what birds have vanished one by one,
Yet knows its boughs more silent than before:
I cannot say what loves have come and gone,
I only know that summer sang in me
A little while, that in me sings no more.

> The form Millay has chosen is the **Italian** or **Petrarchan sonnet**, which is divided into an **octave** of eight lines followed by a **sestet** of six lines. Both the ideas and rhyme scheme will change at the **volta**, or turn, between the two parts. Millay uses a simple, regular **rhyme scheme** in the **octave**: abba / abba.

> In the **sestet**, the rhyme scheme changes to the more subtle and complex: cde / dce, including the **half-rhyme** or **eye-rhyme** of 'one' / 'gone'.

Millay wrote this poem after the First World War. The subject relates to her nostalgia for the happy and thoughtless time before the war, when she had many lovers. Now, many of these young men are dead and she feels sad and lonely. She regrets not appreciating them while they lived.

Questions

1 In the **octave** (lines one to eight), the poet focuses on the **sense of touch**. Which words and phrases particularly evoke ideas of touch?
2 Which expressions in the octave contribute to a **mood** of sadness and regret?
3 The words 'what', 'where' and 'why' dominate the opening line. What do you think these add to the **mood** of the poem?
4 The poet mentions the 'rain' in line three. What does this reference to the weather contribute to the **atmosphere** of the poem?
5 Whom do you think are the 'ghosts' tapping on the window (line four)?
6 In the **sestet**, the poet presents the **image** of 'a lonely tree' that the birds have gradually deserted. What might this image symbolise?
7 How does the poet appeal to the sense of **sound** in the sestet, and how does it illustrate her themes of loss and sadness?

Drafting and redrafting

Most poets spend a great deal of time redrafting and perfecting their work. If you look at the original manuscripts of well-known poems, it is fascinating to see how the poets edited and amended their verses in order to achieve exactly the effect they were aiming at.

If you have studied Wilfred Owen's famous poem 'Dulce et Decorum Est', you may be surprised to see how different his earlier drafts were. The opening lines as published today are shown on the following page, alongside an earlier draft.

'Dulce et Decorum Est'

Bent double, like old beggars under sacks,

Knock-kneed, coughing like hags, we cursed through sludge,

Till on the haunting flares we turned our backs,

And towards our distant rest began to trudge.

5   Men marched asleep. Many had lost their boots,

But limped on, blood-shod. All went lame, all blind;

Drunk with fatigue; deaf even to the hoots

Of tired, out-stripped five-nines that dropped behind.

Gas! GAS! Quick, boys! – An ecstasy of fumbling

10   Fitting the clumsy helmets just in time;

But someone still was yelling out and stumbling,

And flound'ring like a man in fire or lime.

Dim, through the misty panes and thick green light,

As under a green sea, I saw him drowning.

15   In all my dreams, before my helpless sight,

He plunges at me, guttering, choking, drowning.

Owen originally dedicated his poem to 'a certain Poetess', namely, Jessie Pope. Jessie Pope wrote rousing, patriotic verse portraying war as a glorious game and urged young men to 'do their bit'. Owen was bitterly critical because he had first-hand experience of the horror of the trenches. He thought better of denouncing Miss Pope publicly, however, and removed the ironic dedication, which would have compromised the dignity of the sentiments and lessened the universal power of their application.

Look at the changes Owen made between his manuscript draft (itself edited) and the version printed above it, which is the poem as he submitted it for publication. Consider why he made these changes and what they contribute to the ultimate effect of the poem, which many regard as one of the most powerful in the English language.

A word on plagiarism

Although you have been looking at the techniques used by professional writers, it is only their techniques that you may use. You must be careful not to copy the actual writing, a form of theft known as plagiarism.

A few years ago, a young writer from Cornwall was discovered to have imitated the work of some Scottish writers much too closely.

Look at the following two poems, taken from an article in the *Scotsman*. The one on the left is by the Scottish poet Derick Thomson; the one on the right is by the plagiarist.

On Glasgow Streets	**Boscawen Street**
When I hear	When I hear
Glasgow waitresses	seasonal Truro waitresses
talking earnestly	talking earnestly
about Perry Como	about 'Neighbours'
5 or Starsky and Hutch,	5 or Mel Gibson
or singing a song	or singing the number one,
by John Lennon,	I remember
I remember that Wallace	that Flamank
is out the window,	is just out of the window,
10 and Alasdair Mac Colla	10 and Joseph is
at the mill of Gocam-go	at St Keverne,
and my country, for lack of will,	yet my country, for lack of will,
has gone to hell.	has gone to hell.

In this example, the plagiarist has replaced Scottish names with Cornish ones, such as Truro for Glasgow, and he has also updated some of the references to celebrities and TV programmes to more modern ones.

In other respects, however, the poem is identical. It would have been acceptable for the Cornish writer to have used the theme of the loss of local identity, and even to have written a poem in free verse about it, but he has blatantly copied the structure and entire lines and phrases from the original.

The work of the Orkney writer George Mackay Brown was also plagiarised by the same person. Again, this comes from the article in the *Scotsman*. Mackay Brown's work is on the left.

What a boring day it had been in Norday school!	What a boring day it had been in Tollowarn school!
Usually Thorfinn liked history…	Usually Yowann liked history…
But Mr Simon took all the enchantment out of history, with his long lists of the kings of Scotland and the battles that Scotland had either magnificently won or been gloriously defeated in, together with their dates.	But Mr Bedford took all the enchantment and magic out of history, with his long lists of the kings of Cornwall and the battles that the Cornish had either magnificently won or been gloriously defeated in, together with their dates.

This example is even closer to the original. He has simply changed the names; adding an extra phrase 'and magic' is not acceptable as a means of making it into an original piece.

The plagiarist's books were withdrawn from sale. Your award in English will be at stake, however, if you copy someone else's work!

You may develop ideas you find in other writers' work, and you may try some of the techniques they use, but you must never copy work directly like this with just small 'cut-and-paste' alterations.

IMAGINATIVE WRITING: WRITING IN PROGRESS

Here is an example of a piece of imaginative writing progressing through the stages that were outlined on pages 16–36. The candidate initially chose the prose fiction genre, but as her ideas developed her final piece came closer to personal/reflective in effect – even though it was imagined, and not an account of an actual experience. Such a change does not matter: the aim is to produce the best piece of writing possible.

Look at the different steps that led to the final piece of writing. Once you have read the final draft, discuss the questions that follow.

Jackie's imaginative writing

Stage one: outline

Genre: Prose fiction

Setting: A real place – Portencross, near West Kilbride, Ayrshire

Theme: An incident at the harbour – an accident and a rescue

Characters: Girl and her father (based on me and Dad)

Style: First-person narrative; linear structure

Teacher's comment:

This looks fine. The real-life setting should help make the story convincing, as will basing the characters on real people.

(Jackie explained that since her parents split up she would go to her Dad's holiday home at Portencross once or twice a year. She loved the area and knew it well.)

Stage two: plan

- Intro: staying at Dad's holiday house – decision to go for a morning walk.
- Describe lovely weather and scenery.
- Visit the harbour – describe activity – fishermen.
- Someone falls in – Dad and I help with the rescue.
- We get home, wet but happy that all ended well.

Teacher's comment:

This structure seems clear – try writing a first draft.

Stage three: first draft

The first draft began like this:

> One day, when I was spending the weekend with my Dad at his holiday home, I decided to take a walk along the beach. The sun was shining from the moment I woke up. I felt its warmth on my eyelids and at once I felt I must get outdoors and have some vigorous exercise. I asked Dad if he would like to come along, although in some ways I would rather have gone on my own. He said he would come with me as he, too, wanted some fresh air.

Teacher's comment:

Unfortunately, the first draft was rather uneven. The opening was rather stilted. The next sections, describing the walk and the harbour, were better, but those describing the accident and the rescue were melodramatic and did not ring true. Jackie said she had never seen such an event, but she had often been out for walks with her Dad, and she really enjoyed their times together. After discussion, Jackie decided to omit the part about the rescue altogether, even though it had been her original idea, and concentrate instead on creating a happy mood and developing her descriptive writing. She also rewrote her introduction.

Stage four: final draft

> **Morning Walk**
>
> As I began to wake, I could hear the sound of the seagulls wailing and the sun was warm on my eyelids and glowing red. I opened my eyes, screwing them up against the brightness, and went over to look out of the window. The sea glistened with the reflection of the sun. It was a really beautiful morning and I decided to go out for a walk. I planned to take the path along the beach as I felt like some vigorous exercise. I asked my father if he would like to come along, although in some ways I would rather have gone on my own. He agreed the lovely morning was too good to waste, and decided that he, too, would enjoy some fresh air.
>
> The moment he said that I felt glad, as we do not often spend much time together. My parents split up when I was just eight, and I now only see my father occasionally. At first, immediately after the split, I saw him every weekend, but his work takes him abroad frequently, and my visits to him at his holiday home on the coast are now really quite rare.
>
> We cut across the golf course together and then made our separate ways down on to the beach. We walked in a happy silence for what seemed like ages and then we decided to go to Portencross, which is a beautiful little fishing hamlet near where we used to live. Portencross is a rather special place to me. Often, when I was sad in the difficult days when my parents were constantly arguing, I'd go there for some tranquillity and thinking time. There are only a few people living there and an old half-ruined castle. →

→

My father and I walked round the castle. We found an old cannon that was now mostly covered by the tall grass, which was sadly strewn with litter. We tidied the area up a bit while he told me more of the great kings and queens that used to visit here. He loves history, and has an amazing fund of these stories. We looked out towards the now unsafe pier, which boasts of having had some famous boat anchor there on its last trip – although I can't now remember its name.

Normally we would have climbed up the hill to see the breathtaking view of Arran – on a very clear day, if you are lucky, you can also see Ben Nevis and the Heads of Ayr – but that day we didn't. I was still a little apprehensive about climbing the hill after having been chased down it recently by the landlord's goat!

As we walked through the hamlet, the fishing boats were getting ready to ship out. We watched them gather their nets and floats while being pestered constantly by the seagulls that were trying to get at the bait. The sun must have been making them so lazy that they didn't want to catch their own food. My father recognised one of the fishermen and went to talk to him. I continued walking and we arranged to meet up later.

I decided to go to my special seat, which is a column of rocks that forms a type of gate leading to Hunterston Castle. My special seat is a flat area of rock where you can see Bute. It isn't very high up, although it is very sheltered. At this time of year the sea pinks – fragrant pink flowers that I used to pick when I was a little girl – were blossoming and I picked a big bunch of them for old times' sake.

When I eventually came down, my father was already waiting for me. We walked on, past 'murder cottage', which was so called because of a grisly murder committed there a long time ago. It used to always fill me with dread, and even now I felt myself give a little shudder. As we walked on towards the Hunterston power station, the sun disappeared and the sky began to darken suddenly and ominously.

We decided to head back for home, which was at least an hour away. As we walked back, the inevitable happened and it began to rain torrentially. I only had a T-shirt and jeans on, as did my father, and we were soaked through in minutes. This struck us as incredibly funny as the rain plastered our hair down on our heads until we looked like a pair of drowned rats. The sea rose and swirled against the rocks. We could sense the power of the sea and were thankful we were not adrift somewhere with the fishermen.

We arrived home drenched to the skin, still laughing. The storm had ended and the sun was trying to break through the clouds again. My father told me to go and change, and when I had done so there was a mug of hot chocolate waiting. And there, sitting in the middle of the table, was a vase with my sea pinks in it.

Jackie's piece of writing is well within the 1,300-word limit. Do you feel its length is 'appropriate to purpose'?

In groups or pairs, discuss the following questions:

1 How effective do you find the opening paragraph?
2 How effective do you find the ending?
3 What do you feel are the strengths of this piece?
4 Can you identify any weaknesses?
5 What mark would you give this piece out of 15?

From National 5 to Higher

A piece of creative/imaginative writing at Higher will exhibit the following strengths:

- A high degree of originality and evidence of vivid imagination.
- Confident command of the chosen genre.
- Striking and skilful use of the appropriate conventions and linguistic features of the genre.
- A strong focus on purpose and audience.
- Effective and varied expression.
- An effective structure which enhances the purpose/meaning.
- It will approach the limit of 1,300 words (depending on the chosen genre).

By contrast, if a creative piece exhibits features such as the following, it is likely to be inadequate for Higher level:

- It has limited originality or imaginative flair.
- It has limited use of the linguistic features or conventions of the chosen genre.
- It uses language which is not consistently effective.
- Its structure is of limited effectiveness.
- It is considerably short of 1,300 words (depending on the chosen genre).

PART TWO

BROADLY DISCURSIVE WRITING
ARGUMENTATIVE WRITING

The second of the two pieces of writing for your portfolio must be discursive. You may choose either to write an argumentative piece, exploring different views on a topic, or to write a one-sided argument presenting a persuasive case. Alternatively, you may write a report.

Getting started

You will do well at this kind of writing if you:

- are well informed about what is going on in the world
- have strong opinions
- like to argue, or to persuade people
- enjoy working with information or facts
- feel more comfortable writing to a structured paragraph plan.

For discussion

To help clarify your opinions on a particular issue, try this paired discussion exercise.

- Choose a controversial topic or proposal about which people have strong opinions.
- One person should write down three reasons in favour of the proposal.
- The other should write down three reasons against it.
- Now tell each other the three reasons.
- One person should try to persuade the other that he or she has a more convincing case.

For example:

We should help people who are less fortunate than we are.

These people should be working.

Society has a moral duty to look after those in need.

Should we give money to beggars?

They'll just spend the money on drink or drugs.

If you think they will spend the money on drink or drugs you could always buy them some food or a cup of tea.

It's a job for the police or social services, not us.

The ideas that come up in your discussion (or argument!) could then be used to form the basis of a piece of writing.

Try to think of issues on which you personally have strong opinions. For some suggested topics, see pages 79–82.

Researching your topic

Once you have decided what to write about, you should research your topic. The problem here is that there will be too much, rather than too little, source material. It is vital to be selective.

Newspapers, the internet and various source books (such as the *Essential Articles* series, which collects newspaper articles on selected topics) will all provide plenty of ideas.

You should make note of the main arguments and select evidence to back these up.

Practical points to remember

- At the end of a discursive piece of writing, SQA states that you must give 'specific details' of any sources used. This means the dates and writers of newspaper articles; addresses of specific web pages; titles and dates of publication of books. It is not acceptable to say vaguely 'the internet' or 'various newspaper articles'. Remember to note these details when researching your pieces, as it may be difficult to trace them at a later date.

- Footnotes can also be used to acknowledge sources. Laying these out properly will give your writing a professional appearance.

- Make paragraph divisions clear and avoid sub-headings.

- Do not exceed the limit of 1,300 words. Remember that it is possible to gain full marks without using the maximum number of words available.

Planning your answer

A convenient way of gathering your material together is firstly to list points and then to rank them in order of importance.

Objections to your view

Point	Evidence/back-up arguments	Importance

Points supporting your view

Point	Evidence/back-up arguments	Importance

There are many ways to structure and plan your essay. Below, you will find two examples of paragraph plans. Your teacher may provide other suggestions to help you plan your essay.

Paragraph plan (1): the 'for' and 'against' type

Paragraph one

- The opening paragraph should introduce the subject, giving some explanation of why it is important or controversial, and should indicate your own view.

  (Opening paragraphs are looked at in more detail on pages 58–59.)

Paragraph two

- Discuss the opposite view from your own – the side of the argument you find less convincing.

  - Adopt a neutral, unbiased tone:

  > Many people would argue that…
  >
  > Some objectors claim that…

  - Back up each point with evidence. (See pages 59–61 for more on how to use evidence convincingly.)

Paragraph three

- Show why you do not agree with these arguments. This can still be done in a balanced manner without using emotive language. For example:

> While it is true that there is some merit in these arguments, they also have a number of significant weaknesses.

- This section of the essay should then lead into the main part.

Paragraph four onwards

- Put forward convincing arguments for your own view. Remember: don't list your points – link them. This will help to make the essay flow better:

  - Consider the order in which you present your points. Avoid the 'firstly', 'secondly', 'thirdly' approach! This not only makes for a boring piece of writing but also gives no indication of whether one point is of any greater importance than another. An alternative method might be to deal with your points in ascending order (from minor to major), keeping the most convincing argument till the end.
  - Begin each paragraph with a topic sentence that makes it clear how that paragraph relates to the argument as a whole. For example:

> Many incidents over the last few years have given rise to concern.
>
> A considerable amount of evidence exists to demonstrate how serious the problem is.
>
> A number of objections to this view have been put forward.

  - Rhetorical questions can be a useful way of moving from one aspect of a topic to the next, although this technique should not be overused:

> What, then, should the Government do to remedy the situation?

  - Use linking phrases to make it clear how the argument is progressing. For example:

> In addition to this…
>
> In the same way…
>
> It is certainly true that…
>
> Of greater significance is the fact that…
>
> More importantly…
>
> However, perhaps the most compelling argument is…
>
> Therefore, the evidence would suggest that…

Final paragraph

- Sum up the main objections in a balanced way but also make your own position clear.

- If your arguments are structured logically, they will lead naturally to this conclusion. The conclusion should not be a surprise or, even worse, a contradiction of what has gone before.

- If appropriate, you may end with an appeal to the reader in the form of a rhetorical question:

> After all, if we do not tackle the problem now, will it not simply be left as a legacy for future generations to deal with?

Paragraph plan (2): the 'problem' and 'solution' type

An alternative structure for a piece of discursive writing is to:

- outline a problem

- examine solutions that have been attempted

- show why these have not worked, or have only been partially successful

- discuss possible alternative solutions.

In all other respects, a similar approach should be taken to that used in a 'for' and 'against' type of argument:

- Adopt a neutral tone.

- Back up statements with evidence.

- Use linking phrases and topic sentences.

- Grade points in order of importance rather than listing them.

For practice

This short piece of writing is abridged from a longer newspaper article. It illustrates many of the techniques used in discursive writing that we've been looking at. Consider how these techniques are used. While you should not, of course, copy someone else's work, several approaches are used here that you could adapt for use in your own writing.

Stress: have we worried ourselves sick?

If your great-great-grandparents fell through a hole in time and landed here today, they would dance for joy to see the miraculous advances we have made in technology, healthcare and entertainment. But soon they would also begin to wonder why, amid all this amazing stuff, do we look so stressed and anxious?

There is no doubt that our society is technologically and materially far richer than ever before in human history, but our levels of stress, anxiety and depression are also higher than ever. So, too, are our rates of stress-related physical illnesses such as hypertension. The insurer Aviva UK Health says that psychological stress was the primary cause of sickness claims last year. Similarly, a Coventry University study shows that in some parts of the country almost two-thirds of workers say they are suffering from stress-induced depression, while the Health and Safety Executive calculates that in 2008 alone 13.5 million working days were lost to stress, depression and anxiety.

➡

We are worrying ourselves sick. For example, we have proved highly skilled at using technology to stress ourselves and are now overwhelmed by the daily deluge of information – urgent emails, rolling news, celebrity scandal. Mass communication also spreads fear more rapidly than ever before, as can be seen from the global panic over swine flu. The environment we have built around us worsens matters. A study of women randomly assigned to live in flats with a view of nothing but urban sprawl and car parks found that they have far lower mental focus for anything from puzzles to big life challenges, compared to women assigned to flats whose courtyards overlook grass, trees and flowerbeds.

One reason why we seem locked into this spiral of anxiety is the disturbing fact that stress is addictive. Laboratory studies by researchers at the University of Sydney indicate that the more stress you suffer, the more you crave it. We all know that relaxation can calm us, but who has time to sit around doing nothing? We have become manic about speeding things up and must have instant gratification. The multimedia retailer QVC says that a survey of 2,000 UK shoppers found that 47 per cent had suffered 'queue rage', with a fifth having stormed out of a shop after queuing for three minutes or less.

How, then, are we to break free from the cycle? Most of us do know how to relax, but we feel under pressure to keep striving our way out of the problem rather than taking our foot off the pedal. We must learn to step back and commit to giving ourselves a break. We must learn to enjoy relaxing and restorative activities purely for their own sake. After all, just adding 'relaxation anxiety' to our list of worries is hardly going to help.

Adapted from an article by John Naish, © The Times and 13 February 2010 / nisyndication.com

Thinking it over…

Identify examples of the following techniques in the article on stress:

- Rhetorical question
- Topic sentence
- Statement
- Evidence
- Linking words/phrases.

Now look at the structure of the article. Summarise what each paragraph contributes to the development of the argument. (One has been done for you.)

Paragraph	Summary
1	
2	
3	This paragraph develops the topic sentence 'We are worrying ourselves sick' by giving examples of how people create more stress for themselves.
4	
5	

The opening paragraph

The opening paragraph is the most important one. It should:

- catch the reader's attention
- outline the subject under discussion
- give some indication of why the subject is important or controversial
- give clues as to how the rest of the essay will develop.

Many different techniques can be used to achieve these aims:

- An anecdote: a story illustrating a point.
- A rhetorical question that will be answered in detail in the course of the discussion.
- A quotation, such as the opinion of an expert.
- A striking or shocking statistic that draws attention to the extent of a problem.
- A controversial statement that will arouse strong feelings on the part of the reader.

Here are two examples of good openings, written by professional journalists.

Michael Hogan on karaoke

Love it, loathe it or like to make it illegal, karaoke is inescapable. It pops up at weddings, parties, bar mitzvahs. It's become an essential part of the office outing or hen weekend. And now there's a new breed of karaoke bar serving cocktails to stylish crooners. Karaoke tents are also being pitched at most of the summer festivals. There's even an initiative to teach it in primary schools backed by Lord Lloyd Webber. Karaoke is hilarious and brings out the secret show-off in us all. It's also liberating, life-affirming and highly addictive.

Extract from an article in the Daily Telegraph

Note the strong opening sentence, which uses alliteration to catch the reader's attention and makes a bold statement. The next few sentences elaborate on this by showing how widespread karaoke is. The last two sentences make the writer's opinion clear.

Gareth Edwards on swearing

Hundreds of years ago it was deemed an offence against God, and anyone with a 'dirty' mouth risked having their tongue burned out as punishment. Nowadays, bad language is so commonplace most people probably struggle to even raise an eyebrow – unless someone uses the most offensive language possible in the most inappropriate place. So has swearing really lost the power to shock, or have we all just decided that, bad or good, it is just language?

Extract from an article in the Scotsman

In the first two sentences, the writer makes a simple contrast between 'then' and 'now'. Some suspense is created in the opening statement as the subject is not defined but simply referred to as 'it'. The last sentence raises the two sides of the question that will be debated in the rest of the article.

For practice

Here are five different students' attempts to start a piece of writing on the subject of stress. Several of them have used material from John Naish's article on pages 56–57, but they have not necessarily done so in an effective manner. Consider how successful each introduction is and make bullet-point notes. The first one has been started for you.

Introduction	How far does it fulfil the purpose of an introduction? Are any specific techniques used? Are there any problems with this introduction?
1 If your great-great-grandparents fell through a hole in time and landed here today, they would dance for joy to see the miraculous advances we have made in technology, healthcare and entertainment. But soon they would also begin to wonder why, amid all this amazing stuff, do we look so stressed and anxious?	• Amusing picture in words acts as a 'hook' to draw in the reader
2 The insurer Aviva UK Health says that psychological stress was the primary cause of sickness claims last year. A Coventry University study, meanwhile, shows that in some parts of the country almost two-thirds of workers say they are suffering from stress and depression. The Health and Safety Executive calculates that in 2008 alone 13.5 million working days were lost to stress, depression and anxiety.	
3 One of the biggest problems facing everybody today is stress. In this essay I will examine how widespread the problem of stress is. I will discuss the causes of stress and will go on to discuss ways of dealing with the problem.	
4 'Stress,' says journalist John Naish, 'is something we catch from each other like a virus.' The problem is all around us and there is convincing evidence to suggest that it has a serious effect on the country's economy, on family life and on people's health. Nevertheless, while it would be neither realistic nor desirable to expect a completely stress-free existence, there are a number of practical steps that can be taken to make stress more manageable.	
5 In today's society we are literally worrying ourselves sick. For example, our technology is more advanced than ever before but the information overload – like endless emails – is too much for us to take in and leaves us confused and stressed. On the other hand, some people thrive on stress and others use relaxation techniques and breathing exercises to cope with it. However, millions of working days are lost every year because of stress.	

Developing your paragraphs: topic sentences and evidence

In discursive writing, many paragraphs will begin with a topic sentence that makes a statement. You must then develop this, using evidence, in the rest of the paragraph.

For example:

> There is convincing evidence to suggest that watching television is harmful to people's health.

This is a topic sentence. What would you expect the rest of the paragraph to contain?

For practice (1)

The following sentences might be used in a discussion of the influence of television.

Questions

1 Decide which ones are **statements** and which ones are **evidence**.

	Statement	Evidence
1 Recent research shows that spending too many hours per day watching television can have harmful effects on a child's intellectual development.		
2 A twenty-year-old man who watches television for three hours a day until he reaches the age of seventy will have spent as many as six years and three months of his life on this activity.		
3 Some studies suggest that excessive viewing is a factor in conditions such as autism and attention deficit disorder.		
4 Others would argue that television can in fact contribute to the development of intelligence.		
5 One of the most obvious negative effects of TV on the younger generation is a greater reluctance to take exercise.		
6 It has been estimated that in 1993 the average child viewing television in the USA saw programmes that contained a total of 10,000 murders, attacks and other violent acts. By 1997, that number had increased to 12,000.		
7 A study carried out at an American university concluded that men who watch television for three or more hours per day are twice as likely to be obese as those who spend less than an hour a day in front of the screen.		
8 Some academics believe that the influence of television on the younger generation is such an important issue that they have recommended that the effects of screen violence on children should be dealt with as a public health matter in the same way as other topics such as advice on road safety and healthy eating.		

2 Which of these examples could be used as the topic sentence for the start of a paragraph? What do you think these paragraphs would go on to talk about next?

As can be seen from the examples in the table, evidence may take various forms:

- A combination of facts and opinions.
- Anecdotal evidence, consisting of illustrations or stories.
- Statistics, providing evidence of the extent of a problem or of changing trends.
- The views of experts and specialists involved in the field, providing informed, authoritative opinions.

For practice (2)

Read the following newspaper article and answer the questions below.

How doubts about global warming are on the rise...

Global warming scepticism is rising, a major poll shows.

It found that 78 per cent of Britons believe the world's climate is changing, compared to 91 per cent five years ago.

Researchers said the growing doubts have been fuelled by the coldest winter in three decades and the row over leaked emails from the University of East Anglia's Climatic Research Unit.

These appeared to show that scientists manipulated data on temperature records, although two inquiries ruled out malpractice.

The Ipsos Mori survey of 1,822 people for Cardiff University found that 40 per cent believe the seriousness of global warming is exaggerated.

But the vast majority believe in climate change, and believe that human activity is to blame.

Only 18 per cent thought it was mainly or entirely caused by natural processes.

Almost two-thirds would be willing to cut their energy use to help tackle the problem, and 40 per cent would pay significantly more for energy-efficient products.

Professor Nick Pidgeon, of Cardiff University, said the fall in belief in climate change could be down to people's 'finite pool of worry' and greater concern with the financial crisis.

He added: 'The short-term effects are more obvious – the emails, and the fact we had a very cold winter – and people think "where is global warming when we're sitting here in 3 feet of snow?"'

Extract from an article in the Daily Mail

Questions

1. Two sentences in this article perform the function of topic sentences, introducing a point that is then developed in detail. Quote these two sentences.
2. Quote an expression that shows the writer is adopting a balanced, unbiased approach.
3. Quote an example of statistical evidence. What point does it prove?
4. In your own words, summarise two reasons why Professor Nick Pidgeon thinks people are less likely to believe in global warming.

PERSUASIVE WRITING

An argumentative essay examines both sides of an issue; a persuasive essay argues the case for one side only.

As a result, a more personal approach can be adopted: the writer is not trying to be neutral and balanced. If you feel passionately about an issue, it might be a good idea to try a persuasive essay.

To prepare for this task, you would need to undertake similar research to that required by a 'for/against' or 'problem/solution' style of writing.

Where appropriate, however, the style of a persuasive essay can make use of an informal or light-hearted tone in an effort to convince the reader to share the writer's opinion.

Television presenter James May frequently uses this kind of approach in his journalism. Here, he argues that the popular slot-racing game Scalextric is ideal for teaching children about engineering and science.

'Lessons in Scalextric'

Scalextric, which many people will imagine to be a motor-racing toy of some sort, is actually an arena of serious scientific inquiry.

A great deal of stuff that was rendered unnecessarily dull in third-year physics could have been made extremely interesting if all the smelly Victorian apparatus still kicking around our lab had been replaced with a Scalextric set.

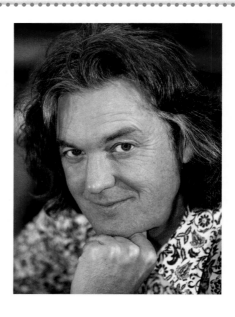

Starting at the wall, it can be demonstrated that mains AC electricity, which can blow your head off, can be transformed and rectified, by the simple expedient of winding wires and arranging diodes, into a 12V DC supply in a connector that can safely be inserted in your ear. Kids should try this.

And now we're off, as Murray Walker might say. I know how a basic electric motor works because I looked inside a Scalextric car, and Fleming's left-hand rule (or was it his right?) is simply more interesting when it's dictating which way around the track you go.

Gearing: it's a dull concept as numbers, but strangely engrossing when it makes the back wheels turn at a manageable speed. The gear whose teeth are at right angles to its circumference is known as a contrate wheel. I know, because it's in the Scalextric instructions.

So much can be learned with this supposed 'toy'. Newton's equations of motion can be demonstrated with a stupid wooden trolley and a ticker-tape machine, or with a ball-bearing falling from the top of a retort stand, but why not use Scalextric? At the end you will not only understand all this stuff, you will also have performance figures for your car.

A body travelling on a curved path is always accelerating towards the centre of its radius. Yawn. You will crash going around the corners for the same reason, and that's just much more interesting. Even the mysteries of geometry can be revealed with Scalextric. The variety of circuits that can be created is infinite, yet there have only ever been twelve basic track sections.

Materials science, friction, the difference between mass and weight – there's as much to learn in Scalextric as there is in a space programme, which is why I think Scalextric should be on the curriculum.

So does Scalextric, as it turns out. This month sees the launch of Scalextric 4 Schools, which will offend the English department but is designed to rekindle the flagging enthusiasm of the nation's youth for engineering and technology. Schools will compete internally, locally and ultimately at a national level to see who can design and build the best car in terms of performance and product development.

Of course we tried to build Scalextric cars in the olden days, but all we really had to hand was Araldite. There are heirlooms in the May household still inadvertently cemented together for eternity with the stuff. We worked out our ideas on graph paper.

Today's kids are given a CAD/CAM program pre-loaded with a basic car design. Because it's on a computer, the 12-year-olds I met were very happy to begin improving it immediately. 'It's too tall,' said one. 'That means the centre of gravity will be too high and it will fall off on the bends.' The country is in safe hands.

What really impressed me, though, was the equipment these pillars-of-society-in-waiting had at their disposal: laser cutters, computer-numeric milling machines, stereolithography machines for rapid prototyping in resin, vac-form plastic moulding machines for low-cost series production of bodies. The only off-the-peg components needed were the motors, axles and wheels, and even General Motors shares that sort of thing. This wasn't a high-fee school attended by the children of rock stars and Russian aristocrats; it was just a normal state operation.

I was amazed. I grew up at the end of the era in which designs had to be drawn on paper and then interpreted by patternmakers and toolmakers before anything could actually be made. Today's students of manufacturing science are learning that the data that creates the design is also used to drive the machinery that makes the parts.

I don't want to fall into the trap of saying that kids these days don't realise how lucky they are, but they don't.

And at the end of it all, they can have a race. There was a book at my school called *Science is Fun!*, but of course it wasn't. This project shows that fun can be scientific, which is much more educational. I was pretty glad when I left school, but if this sort of thing had been going on you'd never have dragged me away from the place.

Please, sir, can I have some more?

Article © Telegraph Media Group Limited 2010

For practice (1): content

- Find one sentence in the article that sums up the writer's aim.
- Find three examples of how scientific principles can be learned through using Scalextric.
- How far does James May's argument convince you?

For practice (2): technique

James May uses a variety of different techniques in this article, such as:

a) contrasting sentence lengths
b) technical jargon
c) irony
d) conversational style
e) self-mockery
f) reference to his personal experience
g) exaggeration (hyperbole)
h) rhetorical question
i) combination of informal and technical language in the same sentence or paragraph
j) factual statement
k) expression of personal opinion.

Question

Look at the following extracts from the article and decide which of the above techniques are being used. (In many of the extracts, more than one language feature is likely to be present.)

1 Starting at the wall, it can be demonstrated that mains AC electricity, which can blow your head off, can be transformed and rectified, by the simple expedient of winding wires and arranging diodes, into a 12V DC supply in a connector that can safely be inserted in your ear. Kids should try this.

2 And now we're off, as Murray Walker might say. I know how a basic electric motor works because I looked inside a Scalextric car, and Fleming's left-hand rule (or was it his right?) is simply more interesting when it's dictating which way around the track you go.

3 Gearing: it's a dull concept as numbers, but strangely engrossing when it makes the back wheels turn at a manageable speed. The gear whose teeth are at right angles to its circumference is known as a contrate wheel. I know, because it's in the Scalextric instructions.

4 Newton's equations of motion can be demonstrated with a stupid wooden trolley and a ticker-tape machine, or with a ball-bearing falling from the top of a retort stand, but why not use Scalextric?

5 A body travelling on a curved path is always accelerating towards the centre of its radius. Yawn.

6 Schools will compete internally, locally and ultimately at a national level to see who can design and build the best car in terms of performance and product development.

7 Of course we tried to build Scalextric cars in the olden days, but all we really had to hand was Araldite. There are heirlooms in the May household still inadvertently cemented together for eternity with the stuff.

8 I was amazed. I grew up at the end of the era in which designs had to be drawn on paper and then interpreted by patternmakers and toolmakers before anything could actually be made.

9 I don't want to fall into the trap of saying that kids these days don't realise how lucky they are, but they don't.

10 I was pretty glad when I left school, but if this sort of thing had been going on you'd never have dragged me away from the place.

For practice (3): technique

This is a bit more difficult!

Question

Pick **three** of the examples on the previous page and try to explain **why** James May uses a particular technique. What purpose or effect is he aiming at?

Task

How good is it?

Here is a summary of what the examiners are looking for.

An **argumentative** essay should:

- present a clear and sustained line of thought
- show evidence of full research and appropriate selection from the sources used
- convey an argumentative tone that is measured and reasonable, and yet carries personal conviction
- communicate to the reader a clear sense that the writer has weighed up different aspects of the argument before reaching a conclusion
- make effective use of a number of argumentative techniques.

A **persuasive** essay should:

- persuade the reader to agree with the purpose or point of view of the writer
- usually concern itself with a single topic or issue
- carry a clear sense of conviction – the writer must be persuaded that what they are saying is important if they are seeking to persuade someone else
- make effective use of a number of persuasive techniques.

Here is an SQA examiner's description of the type of essay that would gain top marks in Higher English:

Discursive writing in the top category will be characterised by a strong sense of engagement with the ideas/issues and a sophisticated understanding of them. The line of thought is subtle and sustained.

Easier said than done!

Bearing this in mind, read the following two discursive pieces written by Higher English students. How far do you think they fulfil the examiner's requirements?

Decide what mark you would award each of them out of 15 and write your own marker's comments in the box.

Sample answer 1: Eilish's discursive essay

Should exams be abolished?

As May rolls around, once again students around the country are cramming for their exams. Some will do well, some not so well. Those who get good marks will tend to apply for courses at college or university, aspiring to their ideal jobs. But is this the best measure of intelligence? Can one hour-long exam really determine whether someone is good at a subject?

Some would say yes. Students who have worked hard throughout the year and studied diligently for their exams will do well, and have few problems passing their exams, while those who have not worked will struggle. They believe exams give hard workers a chance to prove themselves and are only a problem for students who do not work sufficiently hard.

However, this approach does not take into account individual circumstances. Working hard all year does not mean a pupil cannot have a bad day. Ironically, the stress placed on pupils to do well is often detrimental to their marks where a pupil would otherwise have got good grades. On the other hand, someone could cram before an exam but put in no effort for the rest of the year then be lucky with the questions that come up and do well. Therefore, exams cannot possibly be seen as a good judge of how clever or hard-working someone is.

Cramming for exams can also be detrimental to health. Pupils often believe they need to cram to do well. This can lead to them becoming tired, stressed and overworked. Overworked, stressed pupils become overworked and stressed adults. This is not ideal for future colleges, universities and employers who are so focused on exam results, or indeed for the pupils themselves.

Aside from the stress exams put pupils under, the very content of exams can mean pupils lack in-depth knowledge of the subjects themselves. Schools gear courses towards passing exams, meaning pupils may only know the bare minimum in order to pass. For example, in languages, pupils focus on reading and writing practice, or on memorising endless lists of vocabulary, but often cannot hold a single conversation or even order food in their foreign language. Pupils merely regurgitate what they have been spoon-fed without really understanding. Constant preparation for exams, teaching only what an exam board has decided pupils should know, is a huge flaw in the education system that must be addressed by those who advocate the current exams as the best system of testing.

Different schools have different standards of teaching. In general, better schools will give more support to pupils and it is easier for them to do well. Some disagree with this idea. They say that even if teaching is sub-standard, if pupils work hard they can teach themselves course material and do well in their exams. However, this could be seen as unfair: other pupils do not need to do this. The gap in teaching standard between so called 'good' and 'bad' schools must be bridged before it can be said that exams are a fair way of testing students from many different backgrounds and many different schools.

Perhaps a partial solution to these problems would be to replace the traditional exam system with a series of small yet rigorous assessments throughout the year. This would relieve some of the pressure on students and allow pupils to have a bad day without this affecting their overall results too badly. It would show that the student has been working hard all year and reduce the need to cram excessively for an exam. Pupils could demonstrate a deeper understanding of concepts learned with more in-depth assessments.

This system would greatly improve the grades, stress levels and ultimately the happiness of both students and teachers.

Strengths:

Weaknesses:

Mark awarded: _____/15

Sample answer 2: Michael's discursive essay

Nature's Nazis

The sun this week has reminded us all of summer. Increasing temperatures, longer days and the imminent holidays are desired by all but like a piper's drone there is an undercurrent of anxiety as Britain's most hated animal returns to its summer home. The British public have always viewed wasps with an eye of detestation but I think they are one of the most advanced, respectable and tenacious creatures alive, and here's why.

A complaint often made against wasps is that they are useless. They are simply bees that don't make honey and have no necessity in the food chain. However, over fifty species of wasp play a key role in the food chains of many different insects, so the extinction of these 'useless' creatures could have a dramatic effect, particularly in tropical regions where wasps are found more regularly. And without wasps our houses and gardens would be overrun with spiders, ants and flies, so we really owe these guys a thank you.

Wasps also have many admirable and unique talents that have aided and ensured their survival since prehistoric times. Wasps are one of the very few animals who make their own place to live. They make hives, which can house thousands of wasps, by chewing wood in their mouths until it turns into paper, which they can bind together and leave to harden. This process is even more impressive when you consider how long it took for humans to make paper, even though it was being created right in front of us. Obsolete, eh?

And it is not just in the paper-making department that we humans are bested by wasps. Wasps' main food source is sugar, which they can smell from five miles away – sugar doesn't even have a smell! Not only can they detect food from this distance, once it has been located they organise flight paths from their hives – so when you see wasps infesting a bin it is the same wasps who were there the day before and the same ones who will be there tomorrow.

We respect wasps not only for their talents but also for their lifestyle – 'cos these guys really know how to party. Near the end of their lives, post-reproduction and as summer flies away, the wasps gorge on rotting, fermenting apples and thus spend their final days fat, lazy and drunk. Is there any better way to go?

Despite these qualities, wasps remain an abhorred outlaw, feared by many because of their nasty stings. Along with almost everyone else, I have experienced a wasp sting but I came out from it with more than just a red mark – I had a revelation. I pictured myself as the wasp, and vice versa, and realised the immense bravery that these tiny creatures must possess to attack an animal as big as a human. And it is not only bravery that encapsulates the wasp but also ferocity and aggression. Wasps are one of the very few animals who attack simply through anger, and I believe it is this rage and passion to inflict pain that has led to wasps killing more people per year than sharks, alligators, lightning, jellyfish, spiders and scorpions put together. They also have vendettas, so if you feel you have gained a victory over one after you annoy it and it flies off, don't celebrate too soon. That specific wasp has effectively tagged you and will recognise you if you cross paths again, and perhaps next time you won't be so lucky. A wasp's life is focused on violence from the very beginning. A female wasp can lay her eggs inside a caterpillar so that when the eggs hatch the cute baby wasps can eat the caterpillar alive from the inside out, causing a slow but painful death.

Perhaps the aggression of the wasp is what has tempted many sports teams from all over the world to use these creatures in their team name. NBA basketball team the New Orleans Hornets and English rugby's London Wasps are two teams that have certainly done justice to their inspiration through their fast-paced play and attacking mindset. Perhaps the connotations of fear associated with wasps and their yellow and black colours have contributed to these teams being among the most successful in their respective leagues.

As you can see, my opinion of wasps could be deemed as controversial but after learning the black and yellow facts about these wonderful creatures I can't see how anyone can't respect them. They may seem like nature's Nazis at first, but when you really get to know them there is a lot we can learn from these creatures about teamwork, perseverance and passion. When you take into account their miraculous abilities, then you really can't deny that these are, indeed, incredible insects.

Task

Strengths:

Weaknesses:

Mark awarded: _____/15

REPORT WRITING

The third discursive variation is report writing. The SQA offers the following advice on this:

- The report must contain relevant complex information selected from at least two sources.
- The material drawn from sources must be recast or paraphrased in a way that is appropriate to the purpose.
- The report must fulfil a clearly expressed remit; it must be prefaced by a concise statement outlining its purpose and describing the procedures used to gather information.
- The writing should have a logical structure.
- Attention should be given to linking the various aspects of the report.
- Diagrams, tables, charts and graphs may be included if appropriate. Headings, appendices, bibliographies, and a lettering or numbering system may be used to separate sections of the report. (You should never do this in an essay, however.)

A factual, impersonal and unemotive tone is the most appropriate for this exercise. If you like to write in a humorous or personal style, don't select the report option!

Warning!

Don't regard a report as an easy option. A 'cut-and-paste' approach will not be acceptable here: the need for logically structured writing applies to report writing just as much as it does to argumentative and persuasive writing.

For practice

In the box on pages 70–71 is some source material that could be used for a report on the subject of alcohol. The extracts come from www.drinkaware.co.uk and http://www.gov.scot/Topics/Health/Services/Alcohol, but there are many other similar sources on this topic.

Use the information here, plus some research of your own, to construct a report on the problem of alcohol.

First, draw up a paragraph plan. For example:

- The extent of the problem.
- Effects of alcohol on:
  - health
  - the economy
  - society.
- Steps that could be taken to improve the situation.

Next, select relevant information for each paragraph.

Finally, write an introductory paragraph outlining the purpose of the report.

What is binge drinking?

The NHS definition of binge drinking is drinking heavily in a short space of time to get drunk or feel the effects of alcohol.

Around 40 per cent of patients admitted to A&E are diagnosed with alcohol-related injuries or illnesses, many of which result from binge drinking.

The amount of alcohol someone needs to drink in a session for it to be classed as 'bingeing' is less clearly defined, but the marker used by the NHS and the National Office of Statistics is drinking more than double the daily recommended units of alcohol in one session.

The Government guidelines state that men should not regularly drink more than three to four units a day, and women should not regularly exceed two to three units daily.

Binge drinking for men, therefore, is drinking more than eight units of alcohol – or about three pints of strong beer. For women, it's drinking more than six units of alcohol, equivalent to two large glasses of wine.

What are the effects of binge drinking?

Some studies show that drinking a large amount of alcohol over a short period of time may be significantly worse for your health than frequently drinking small quantities.

Getting very drunk can affect your physical and mental health:

• Accidents and falls are common because being drunk affects your balance and co-ordination. You're also more likely to suffer head, hand and facial injuries. Binge drinking has also been linked to self-harm.

• In extreme cases, you could die. Overdosing on alcohol can stop you breathing or stop your heart, or you could choke on your vomit.

• Nearly a third (29 per cent) of alcohol-related deaths are a result of alcohol-related accidents. These deaths are more common among 16- to 34-year-olds.

• Binge drinking can affect your mood and your memory, and in the longer term can lead to serious mental health problems.

More commonly, binge drinking can lead to antisocial, aggressive and violent behaviour.

Alcohol is a factor in:

• one in three (33 per cent) sexual offences

• one in three (33 per cent) burglaries

• one in two (50 per cent) street crimes.

Binge drinking is most common among 16- to 24-year-olds, and is more common among men than women. The General Lifestyle Survey 2008 showed that 21 per cent of men and 14 per cent of women drank more than double their recommended units on at least one day in the previous week. However, in the last decade binge drinking among young British women has increased rapidly.

And binge drinking when you're young can become a habit. Studies have shown that those who drink a lot in their teens and early 20s are up to twice as likely as light drinkers to be binge drinking 25 years later.

Alcohol and Scotland's economy

Alcohol misuse places a heavy financial burden on Scottish society.

In 2001, **the direct impact on the economy was estimated to be £766 million**. This figure represents the cost of working days lost, reduced efficiency at work, increased unemployment, early retirement, early death (during working age), workplace accidents and victims of alcohol-related crime.

But the costs don't stop there.

The indirect financial impact of alcohol is currently estimated at £717.7 million a year.

This represents the cost of dealing with alcohol misuse to the NHS (£110.5m), social work (£96.7m), the criminal justice system and the emergency services (£276.7m). There is also a human cost of early deaths among those who are not working (£233.8m).

Although indirect costs may not affect the productivity of the private sector, money spent in this way can't be used for other things – like improving transport or employing more nurses or teachers.

Social effects of alcohol abuse

The local pub or club has been at the heart of many of Scotland's communities for generations. Such establishments provide important opportunities for socialising and spaces for celebrations of all kinds. They are also a source of local employment, as are hotels and, in many rural areas, distilleries.

Despite these benefits, some communities suffer through alcohol misuse. Drunken and antisocial behaviour causes distress to many, especially the elderly and infirm. Younger children can be put off using parks and play areas because of the drunken antics of their elders and the mess they sometimes leave behind.

Meanwhile, alcohol misuse, whether in young people or adults, wastes lives and robs communities and society of productive people who might otherwise make a positive difference to the lives of those around them and to the nation.

From National 5 to Higher

A piece of discursive writing at Higher will exhibit many of the following strengths:

- It will not simply state arguments for and/or against, but will evaluate the strengths and/or weaknesses of these arguments.

- It will grade the arguments in order of importance rather than merely listing them.

- It will back up statements with substantial evidence based on research. For instance, a point will be more convincingly argued if two pieces of evidence, rather than just one, are provided.

- It will employ a variety of types of evidence – anecdotal, statistical, quotations from experts, etc.

- It will convey maturity by showing awareness of the complexity of the issue being discussed. Not all issues divide simply into right versus wrong. Equally, one point could be interpreted differently and used on either side of the argument. For instance, something could be seen as an advantage but, if it were taken too far or used inappropriately, could end up being a disadvantage.

- It will take a consistent approach, both in terms of viewpoint and style of expression. For example, if the approach taken is generally formal and balanced, the style should not suddenly become informal or emotive.

- It will approach the limit of 1,300 words.

By contrast, if a discursive piece exhibits features such as the following, it is likely to be too simple for Higher level:

- It presents a series of for-and-against points in the form of a list without any logical sequencing.

- It presents a series of points without evaluating the relative importance of these (e.g. which ones the writer considers to be the most convincing).

- It does not convey any sense of genuine personal interest in the issue and, particularly in a persuasive piece, a sense of strong personal commitment to a particular point of view.

- It relies on statements of opinion which are not backed up with a variety of different types of evidence.

- It is too dependent on material lifted from research sources that is not properly integrated into the line of argument.

- It falls considerably short of 1,300 words.

PART THREE

SUGGESTED TOPICS FOR WRITING
CREATIVE TOPICS

As explained in the Introduction to this book, the choice of what to write about is your own, although your portfolio must contain two pieces from different genres. One must be broadly creative and the other broadly discursive. The following lists are intended to provide suggestions that will trigger ideas of your own.

Personal/reflective

A personal/reflective piece of writing should reveal something of yourself; your own personality should come across clearly.

1 Me, myself, and I

Reflect on how you see yourself as a person, and compare your own viewpoint with what you imagine to be those of your friends, parents, grandparents, teachers…

2 Memories: looking through the family photo album

For this, you could use certain photographs as triggers for anecdotes about your life or the lives of your relatives. You might, for example, compare the people in old black-and-white photographs with those in present-day images.

3 School: a preparation for life?

Reflect on how well you feel your own education is equipping you for life. This could include a discussion of the relevance of the content of your subjects. It might also take account of the social aspect of a school, and what this teaches you. You might wish to reflect on the vogue for home schooling, and how a child's experience of this might differ from a school-educated child.

4 Why _____ is important to me

Explore the reasons why something – for example, a sport, music, art, animals, family, following fashion – is important in your life. Try to convey both your enthusiasm and your knowledge of the subject, and your reasons for feeling so passionate about it.

5 'I'm glad I'm (not) an only child'

Referring closely to your own situation, and also reflecting on your observations of others, evaluate the advantages of your own position in the family.

6 Travel

Travel is said to broaden the mind. How far do you agree? Discuss what you feel you have learned on your travels. 'Travels' could include family holidays, school trips or just daily travel within a city or through rural areas.

In the novel The Prime of Miss Jean Brodie, *Miss Brodie takes her girls, who attend an exclusive private school in Edinburgh, on a walk through the Grassmarket, then an area of great economic deprivation, in order to open their eyes to how the poor live.*

7 'I'm proud to be Scottish' (or Pakistani, Indian, English, Irish, etc.)

Reflect on how your nationality has affected your life so far, and how patriotic you feel you are.

8 Balancing two cultures

If you belong to an ethnic or cultural minority, describe and reflect on how you have had to reconcile your culture with that of the majority in the country. Try to assess the impact this has had on your life, and whether this has been positive or negative on the whole.

David Daiches' autobiography, In Two Worlds, *tells of his childhood as a Jewish boy growing up in a largely Christian Scotland and attending a Scottish school.*

9 Influences

Explore the various influences that have turned you into the person you are today. This could include family, friends and school, the influence of the media and also factors such as your health or the area where you live.

10 'Heaven and hell'

You could write about this topic either seriously or humorously. A popular newspaper column asks celebrities to reflect on things they love and hate, and you could use this as your structure.

11 Beauty

Reflect on the importance that beauty has in your life. You should think of beauty in its widest sense, not just in terms of human appearance. Reflect on what you consider beautiful, and how important you feel it is to have beautiful things in your life.

Imaginative

Short story/drama script

Imaginative writing may take the form of a complete short story or a chapter of a novel. If your piece of writing takes the form of a chapter, write a note at the beginning explaining that this is your intention.

Most of the following topics could also be adapted into a drama script. Look back at pages 37–41 for advice on how to do this.

1 Write a story based on a theme, for example: love, hate, fate, jealousy, family relationships, rivalry, racism, etc.

2 Write a story with a school setting. The plot might involve: a school dance; a trip; a sports day; a charity fundraising event, such as a fashion show or talent contest; a quarrel or a friendship that changes; peer pressure.

In 'Black Eyes' by Philippa Pearce, a teddy bear provides the focus for some psychological mind games between two small girls. The result is a surprisingly disturbing and suspense-filled story.

3 Write a story in which a family relationship is central.

4 Write a story in which the weather plays a significant part. This could be heat, cold, rain, thunder, storms, etc.

Somerset Maugham gave the title 'Rain' to a story set in the tropics, in which the unending monsoon gradually gets on the characters' nerves.

In Jack London's 'To Build a Fire', set in Alaska, the cold is central to the plight of the main character, who dies after a desperate struggle to survive.

5 Write a story set in a real place that you know well.

6 Write a story set in Scotland. Try to make the setting important or noticeable in some way. You might include some speech in a Scottish dialect, for example.

7 Write the first chapter of a detective/mystery story. Focus on building up atmosphere and end your chapter on a cliffhanger.

8 Choose a well-known proverb as your title, and write a story to illustrate the theme. For example, 'every cloud has a silver lining' or 'birds of a feather flock together'. →

9 Write a story based on Christmas, Hanukkah, Eid or another religious festival.

The story 'Night in Paris' by Patrice Chaplin takes as its theme the practice of 'regifting' – passing on an unwanted Christmas gift to someone else. The story is entertaining because the gifts eventually arrive back with their original donors, but in a slightly battered condition.

10 Write a story involving civilian life during a war.

11 '…the soldier knew someone had blundered.' Write a story involving a military blunder of some kind.

12 Write a story involving two friends who become rivals.

13 Write a story in which someone is persuaded to do something they later regret.

14 Write a story in which the supernatural plays an important role.

15 Write a story in which the generation gap is an important element.

16 Write a story centred round an object: a piece of jewellery, a watch, a photograph, a piece of furniture, a painting, etc.

17 Write a story centred round a family ceremony, such as a funeral, christening or wedding.

18 Write a story focusing on an interesting character: someone old, eccentric, ambitious, etc.

19 Write a modern story with a *Romeo and Juliet* theme.

20 Write a story involving a character returning to a place where they used to live.

'Home' by Iain Crichton Smith tells the story of a man who has become rich and successful returning to the modest tenement home of his youth. He encounters hostility, however, not admiration, from the people who still live there.

Poetry

Poetry is a very personal literary form, and so you could choose virtually any topic about which you have strong feelings. Although some poets have produced humorous poems and narrative poems, you will probably find it easier to write reflectively.

Topics you might choose include:

1 Expression of an emotion. Love has traditionally been the most common trigger, but any emotion could be communicated.

Sylvia Plath wrote her poem 'Morning Song' as an expression of her feelings towards her newborn baby.

Ted Hughes, Plath's ex-husband, wrote a series of poems detailing their relationship, from its joyful beginning to its tragic end (when Plath took her own life). The book is called Birthday Letters.

2 Evoking a mood.

3 Description of a person.

4 Description of a place and the feelings it arouses.

5 Reflections on some aspect of human life, such as birth.

6 Reflections on some aspect of the natural world.

7 Reflections on an incident.

8 Reflections on a social issue, such as war.

9 Reflections on an aspect of human nature.

10 Reflections on a personal experience.

11 Reflections on a brief moment of observation.

12 Reflections on a myth or fable.

It would be very possible to combine some of these ideas successfully.

DISCURSIVE TOPICS

The second requirement of the portfolio is a piece of discursive writing.

In addition to the topics listed below, some of the topics listed under 'personal/reflective' could also be approached, but in a more impersonal way. Ones that would be suitable are those on education (3), the effects of a child's position within the family (5), 'balancing two cultures' (8) and 'heaven and hell' (10). Instead of drawing on your personal experience alone, you could research some facts on these topics and evaluate the evidence.

1 Parents and children
Discuss the problems and difficulties that arise between the generations. What seems to be important in establishing a good relationship?

2 A cyber world
Discuss the advantages and disadvantages of mobile phones, social media and the internet in modern life.

3 The British royal family in the twenty-first century
There was controversy about Prince Harry being on active service in a war zone, and the role of members of the royal family has been much discussed. The behaviour of certain individuals has also attracted criticism for tarnishing the family's image as a whole. Discuss to what extent the royal family still has a valuable role to play in society today.

4 The British armed forces in the twenty-first century
So far this century, the British Army has been deployed in conflict in countries such as Iraq and Afghanistan. Many people feel that Britain should no longer attempt to hold a position on the world stage. Others think that a return to some form of national service would be useful. Discuss the role of the armed forces in Britain today.

5 The Sins of the Fathers
When he was Prime Minister, Gordon Brown apologised for Britain's role in the slave trade, and the German leader Angela Merkel apologised for her country's part in the holocaust. Are we responsible for the past, or for what our ancestors may have done? Should people in the twenty-first century have to apologise for the misdemeanours of their ancestors?

6 Should we condemn adults for bad behaviour in their childhood and teenage years?

Politicians such as David Cameron, Barack Obama and Bill Clinton have all admitted to drug use, and George W. Bush to alcohol abuse. Should this disqualify them from positions of responsibility? Should those with a gaffe-free past be rewarded for their good behaviour?

7 Teenage life in the twenty-first century

A girl invited people to a party via an internet chatroom. Her parents' house was severely damaged and they asked for her to be arrested. Discuss the problems and pressures faced by teenagers of your generation. You might compare them with those faced by earlier generations.

8 Tests and examinations

Some people believe in coursework; others in tests. What is the best way to measure ability? How fair are methods of assessment? Is cheating a factor, for example, downloading and copying material from the internet?

9 The class system

This famous photograph shows some boys from Harrow public school arousing interest at a station.

Consider how far class consciousness survives today. You might consider aspects such as education, lifestyles and careers. Will we ever have a 'classless' society?

10 Religious faith

Discuss the role of religion in modern life. Does it help to maintain good moral standards and order in life? Or does it cause more harm than good in some ways?

11 The size zero debate

Write about the issues of excessive weight loss: the requirement for models to be super-slim; the resistance of the fashion industry to using models of a healthy weight and the efforts to change this; the popularity of very thin celebrities such as Victoria Beckham and Keira Knightley; the health issues.

12 Education

Write about various aspects of education, including single sex education, independent versus comprehensive schools, boarding schools, denominational schools, etc.

13 Fame and celebrity

Some people believe there should be more laws restricting what can be published in the press about the lives of celebrities; others believe it is the price they must pay for the privileges that come with celebrity. Write about the advantages and disadvantages of fame.

14 Money

Discuss the importance of money in life. To what extent does it relate to happiness and wellbeing? Does winning the lottery necessarily lead to a better life?

15 Celebrity adoption

Discuss the rights and wrongs of celebrities such as Madonna and Angelina Jolie adopting children from developing countries like Malawi, particularly if the children have living relatives.

16 Reality television/Talent shows

Explore issues such as the long-term effect on participants, and the values that are put across. Refer to particular programmes, rather than being too general.

17 The sources of charity funds

A convicted paedophile left a large legacy to the Girl Guide movement. There were objections that it was deeply inappropriate for the Guides to accept this, even though the organisation could use the money for good. Members of the Church of Scotland felt that it should turn down lottery funding, because the Church in general disapproves of gambling. Does the end justify the means? Should charities refuse money that has come from a source that is unacceptable to some people?

18 Religious symbols in dress

A teaching assistant was suspended for wearing a niqab (a face veil), but sought legal aid to pursue a grievance. She lost her case in the courts. In France, Muslim girls are not allowed to wear headscarves in school. Women in countries like Saudi Arabia and Qatar must wear a burqa (a full-body gown). Someone working on an airline check-in desk was suspended for wearing a gold cross, on the grounds that it was jewellery. Discuss the ethics of showing religious affiliations through dress.

19 Keeping animals in captivity

Children used to love a day at the zoo because it gave them a chance to ride on an elephant and feed the sea lions. Nowadays, most zoos see their role as preserving endangered species and educating the public rather than providing entertainment. Many zoos do not keep large animals such as polar bears, giraffes or elephants any more because they feel it is cruel to restrict animals that like to wander. This means that many of today's children will never see one of these animals in real life. Evaluate the situation as you see it.

20 The ethics of giving to charity

Should we give to beggars? Some people feel that all handouts to charity should be organised centrally so that we can assess who is most deserving, and the money channelled to where it can do the most good. Some beggars are said to operate a system of intimidation whereby certain individuals claim a right to the most lucrative pitches. Animal charities get far more money than those for neglected children. However, people like to choose for themselves to whom to give. Evaluate the pros and cons of regulating charity donations.

Template 1: Progress log (Creative)

Name _____

		Tick when submitted
Date	Draft title and proposal (enter in full)	Teacher's comments
Date	Outline plan: Teacher's comments	Outline plan: My comments
Date	First draft: Teacher's comments	First draft: My comments
Date	Second draft: Teacher's comments	Second draft: My comments
Date	**FINAL VERSION**	Number of words ☐ Spell-checked (tick) ☐

Template 2: Progress log (Discursive)

Name _____

	Date		Tick when submitted
Draft title and proposal (enter in full)		Teacher's comments	
Outline plan: Teacher's comments	Date	Outline plan: My comments	
First draft: Teacher's comments	Date	First draft: My comments	
Second draft: Teacher's comments	Date	Second draft: My comments	
FINAL VERSION	Date	Number of words [ ]	Spell-checked (tick) [ ]	Sources entered (tick) [ ]

Newspapers: Name of newspaper; date; name of writer
Books: Title; author; date of publication; page numbers
Web pages: Address; writer; date

Template 3: Record of sources (Discursive)

Date	Source	Summary of information

ACKNOWLEDGEMENTS

The Publishers would like to thank the following for permission to reproduce copyright material:

Photo credits

p.vi (t) © Imagestate Media, (c) © Image Source / Getty Images, (b) © Imagestate Media; p.vii (t) © Photodisc / Getty Images, (c) © moodboard – Fotolia.com; p.viii © Stockbyte / Getty Images; p.ix (t) © fred goldstein / Fotolia.com, (c) © Photodisc / Getty Images, (b) © Pieter Bregman – Fotolia.com; p.1 (bl) © Everett Collection / Rex Features, (br) © Associated Newspapers / Daily Mail / Rex Features; p.2 © Rex Features; p.3 © David Hartley / Rex Features; p.4 (t) © David Bebber / The Times / NI Syndication, (b) © Nick Ray / The Times / NI Syndication; p.8 © Geraint Lewis / Rex; p.12 © Eric Gevaert – Fotolia.com; p.13 © Agb – Fotolia.com; p.18 © Rex Features; p.21 © Darren Lyons / Daily Mail / Rex Features; p.22 © Photodisc / Getty Images; p.24 © Photodisc / Getty Images; p.27 © Imagestate Media; p.29 © Photodisc / Photolibrary Group Ltd; p.34 © Tony Buckingham / Rex Features; p.36 © Getty Images; p.37 (t) © Alex Nikada / iStockphoto.com, (b) © INTERFOTO / Alamy; p.38 © TS / Keystone USA / Rex Features; p.39 (t) © Alastair / REX, (b) © Robbie Jack / Corbis; p.40 © Mary Evans Picture Library / Alamy; p.42 © Sam Chadwick / Alamy; p.44 © Underwood & Underwood / CORBIS; p.45 Image from the Bodleian Library, University of Oxford, First World War Poetry Digital Archive, file WOOUEFf318. Reproduced with kind permission of the Trustees of the Owen Estate; p.56 © Imagestate Media; p.60 © Comstock Images / Photolibrary Group Ltd; p.62 © Eddie Mulholland / Rex Features; p.63 © Radharc / Alamy; p.70 © Liv Friislarsen – Fotolia; p.74 © c.20thC.Fox / Everett / Rex Features; p.75 iStockphoto / Ionescu Bogdan Cristian; p.76 © Photodisc / Getty Images; p.78 © Photodisc / Getty Images; p.80 (t) © Imagestate Media, (b) © Getty Images; p.81, © Jason Stitt – Fotolia.com; p.82 © MBI / Alamy.

Chapter opener image reproduced on pages v, 1, 16, 37, 42, 48, 52, 62, 69, 73 and 79 © Getty Images / iStockphoto / Thinkstock

Acknowledgements

p.2 Extract from 'Great escapes: where I go when it's all too much' © *The Times* / News Syndication; p.3 Extract from *How to Kill your Husband* by Kathy Lette, published by Simon and Schuster UK, 2007; p.4 Two extracts from 'Great escapes: where I go when it's all too much' © *The Times* / nisyndication.com; p.7 'The Road Not Taken' from *The Poetry of Robert Frost* by Robert Frost, published by Jonathan Cape. Reprinted by permission of The Random House Group Ltd.; p.8 'What might have been' © Anne Fine, reproduced with kind permission of David Higham Associates; p.12 'Running' © Rebecca Dodds; p.21-4 Extract from 'Mort' by John Wain, published in *You Can't Keep out the Darkness* by Bodley Head Children's Books, 1980. Reprinted with kind permission of the John Wain Estate; p.31 Extract from *The Necklace* by Guy de Maupassant reproduced with kind permission of Wordsworth Editions Ltd; p.33-5 Extract from 'Uneasy Homecoming' by Will F. Jenkins, published in *The Penguin Book of Horror Stories* by Penguin Books Ltd, 1984; p.34 Extract from 'Through the Tunnel' by Doris Lessing, published in *To Room Nineteen* by HarperCollins © HarperCollins Publishers Limited; p.43 'Sonnet XLIII' Copyright © Edna St. Vincent Millay, "What lips my lips have kissed, and where, and why" from *Collected Poems*. 1923, 1951, by Edna St. Vincent Millay and Norma Millay Ellis. Reprinted with the permission of The Permissions Company, Inc., on behalf of Holly Peppe Literary Executor, The Millay Society www.millay.org; p.46-7, Extracts from an article on plagiarism published by the *Scotsman*, 12 May 1999 © The Scotsman Publications Ltd; p.56-7, 59 Extracts adapted from article 'Stress: why are we anxious amid our plenty?' © *The Times* / nisyndication.com; p.61 Extract from article 'How doubts about global warming are on the rise after "big freeze" winter and emails row' in the *Daily Mail* 11 June 2010 © Associated Newspapers Ltd; p.62-3 Extracts from 'Lessons in Scalextric' by James May © Telegraph Media Group Limited 2009; p.67 'Nature's Nazis' © Michael Dodds; p.70 Extract beginning 'What is binge drinking?' from www.drinkaware.co.uk, reproduced with kind permission; p.71 Extract beginning 'Alcohol and Scotland's economy' – Crown copyright material is reproduced under Class Licence Number C02P0000060 with the permission of the Controller of HMSO – 'Alcohol – Our Economy and Community' first published in 2010 by www.infoscotland.com.

Every effort has been made to trace all copyright holders, but if any have been inadvertently overlooked the Publishers will be pleased to make the necessary arrangements at the first opportunity.